THE TERRY LECTURES

The Police and the Public

THE POLICE
AND THE PUBLIC

BY ALBERT J. REISS, JR.

New Haven and London
Yale University Press
1971

Designed by Sally Sullivan
and set in Linotype Times Roman type.
Printed in the United States of America by
The Carl Purington Rollins Printing-Office
of the Yale University Press.

Distributed in Great Britain, Europe, and Africa by
Yale University Press, Ltd., London; in Canada by
McGill-Queen's University Press, Montreal; in Mexico
by Centro Interamericano de Libros Académicos,
Mexico City; in Central and South America by Kaiman
& Polon, Inc., New York City; in Australasia by
Australia and New Zealand Book Co., Pty., Ltd.,
Artarmon, New South Wales; in India by UBS Publishers'
Distributors Pvt., Ltd., Delhi; in Japan by John
Weatherhill, Inc., Tokyo.

The Dwight Harrington Terry Foundation Lectures
on Religion in the Light of Science and Philosophy

The deed of gift declares that "the object of this foundation is not the promotion of scientific investigation and discovery, but rather the assimilation and interpretation of that which has been or shall be hereafter discovered, and its application to human welfare, especially by the building of the truths of science and philosophy into the structure of a broadened and purified religion. The founder believes that such a religion will greatly stimulate intelligent effort for the improvement of human conditions and the advancement of the race in strength and excellence of character. To this end it is desired that a series of lectures be given by men eminent in their respective departments, on ethics, the history of civilization and religion, biblical research, all sciences and branches of knowledge which have an important bearing on the subject, all the great laws of nature, especially of evolution . . . also such interpretations of literature and sociology as are in accord with the spirit of this foundation, to the end that the Christian spirit may be nurtured in the fullest light of the world's knowledge and that mankind may be helped to attain its highest possible welfare and happiness upon this earth." The present work constitutes the thirty-ninth volume published on this foundation.

To
Emma
Peter, Paul, and Amy

CONTENTS

PREFACE

The conventional view of the criminal-justice system provides almost no information on encounters and transactions between police officers and citizens, the microcosm that generates all cases for processing in the criminal-justice system. The core of all these transactions, commencing with those between citizens and the police, is a discretionary decision. The main purpose of my research that began in 1962, was to investigate how citizens decide to mobilize the police and how the police decide to intervene in the affairs of citizens. At the same time, I sought to understand how police and citizens exercise discretion in their transactions and, particularly, how and why they decide not to set the machinery of criminal justice in motion. The legality of police behavior toward citizens was another important subject to explore.

Since so little was known about the transactions between police and citizens, it seemed that field work was the only reasonable way to investigate them. Thus, in 1963 and 1964, I began to ride with the police during their tours of duty. Several graduate students joined me in this form of observation in 1965 and 1966. In this way, more than 200 different tours of duty were observed in Detroit and Chicago.

These studies of the police came to the attention of the National Crime Commission in 1965. The staff of the Commission was especially interested in creating profiles of police precincts, with an emphasis on understanding how police and citizens related to one another in the policing of everyday life. As a result, we agreed to do surveys of police and citizen expectations and conceptions of one another, while, at the same time, studying their actual behavior in encounters. We would thus be able to compare expectations with behavior.

By this time, I was led to conclude that the only way to quantitatively evaluate the information obtained from field observation was to develop schedules whereby the transactions between police and citizens could be systematically observed. In the search for a major unit of recording, it became clear that police work was built around *encounters* with citizens. The encounter is initiated when the police are mobilized to interact with citizens and terminates when the police leave the setting where the encounter took place. We found that we could systematically observe and record the major roles, behavior, and decisions of police and citizens in the encounter.

The purpose of these studies was to generalize about transactions between police and citizens in the United States. Since there seemed to be important differences in the way police departments are organized according to size and location as well as degree of bureaucratization and modernization, we wished to draw a sample from all United States police departments. However, time and the cost of observation necessitated our limiting the investigation to a small number of cities. We chose to study commands in major metropolitan areas only. Three ideal types of police command were selected and the cooperation of their commanders secured. Boston, Massachusetts was chosen to represent the traditional police department based on an ethnic occupational culture (here, the "Irish cop") and personalized administration of the department. Chicago, Illinois was chosen to represent the model of the modern, bureaucratically organized department based on systems analysis and a centralized command and control. Washington, D.C. was selected because the department was in the process of professionalizing the staff and moving toward modernization of its command and control systems.

To reduce the administrative problems in conducting the investigation while at the same time insuring that the encounters selected would be representative of transactions between police and citizens, we made an effort to sample them. This was not easy, since the occurrence of any encounter cannot be predicted in a way that would enable the observer to be present independently of the officer or citizen systems. Clearly, the only way to solve this problem was to tap into the police system by being with the police as encounters arose in the course of their work. However, dependence on the police system not only places limitations on the nature of the observation, but it also poses other problems for observers. Fundamentally, it does not permit the investigator to observe what takes place among the citizens after the police terminate the encounter, although subsequent police behavior may be observed.

Our plan to sample police precincts within each city, to represent major class and race differences and differences in the rate of crime, soon gave way, for reasons of economy, to the deliberate selection of high-crime-rate white and Negro police precincts. We tried to select precincts with a heterogeneous class structure. Dorchester and Roxbury were chosen to represent respectively the high-crime-rate white and black precincts in Boston. Similarly, Fillmore and Town Hall would represent the high-crime-rate black and white precincts in Chicago. The problem of selecting two comparable precincts in Washington, D.C. was more difficult, and ultimately we decided to study four of them so that the variation in crime rates as well as in race and class could be examined more closely.

Since the occurrence of encounters is not predictable, it also is not possible to randomize their selection. Police officers, however, are sworn to duty twenty-four hours a day with a tour of duty lasting eight hours. A probability sample of tours of duty has the effect of randomizing the selection of encounters, since almost all encounters occur during regular tours of duty (although there is some reason to believe that when not assigned to a tour of duty the police give their attention only to the most serious felony situations). Given the fact that the type and frequency of encounters vary by hour, day, and week, tours of duty were selected to represent this variation.

The way the police respond to mobilizations from citizens or intervene in the lives of citizens on their own initiative is organized by the department according to major functions, such as patrol, traffic, and investigation. Except for traffic, most of the policing of everyday life arises during routine patrol. Our observation, therefore, was limited to the mobile and foot patrol.

During the summer of 1966, thirty-six observers rode with the police on eight-hour tours of duty. They recorded their observations immediately afterwards. One schedule was completed for each encounter. Observation lasted for about seven weeks in each city. To examine the effect of an observer's background and training on his observation and to increase confidence in the findings, the twelve observers in each city were selected equally from the areas of law, law enforcement, and social science.

The observers reported on 5,360 mobilizations of the police, of which 28 percent failed to produce any transactions with citizens. Most of the mobilizations, 81 percent, originated with citizens telephoning the police for service and the department dispatching a one- or two-man beat car to handle the incident. Fourteen percent originated on the initiative of police while patrolling an area, and 5 percent originated when a citizen mobilized the police in a field setting. Observers were required to report in detail on all citizens, with a maximum of five, participating in an encounter. They reported in detail on 11,255 citizens.

As observers became familiar with the microcosm of the encounter it became apparent that the relations between police and citizens are problematic in several important respects. Making the objectives of police and citizens in the encounter compatible was complicated by the fact that the immediate problems of citizens are regarded as work and routine by the officers. Moreover, how the police deal with a situation depends largely upon the willingness of the citizenry to be policed. Added to this is the element of uncertainty in all human action which nonetheless is structured by formal and informal sets of expectations on both sides. The fact that we had to rely on police organizations to study the encounters gives the transactions a somewhat one-sided perspective from the work role of the police.

The research that is the underpinning for these lectures is based on many transactions, fiscal and fiducial, with many individuals. Financial assistance was provided by Grant GS 257, National Science Foundation; by Grant Award 006 from the Office of Law Enforcement Assistance, United States Department of Justice; and, by a travel grant from The Russell Sage Foundation. In every community I visited, from as far north as Seattle and Montreal south to Miami and New Orleans, police officials were most generous of their time and provided opportunities for me to collect information and observe operations. Appreciation is expressed to these local police officials, especially O. W. Wilson and Herman Goldstein, then of the Chicago Police Department, who served as faithful counselors.

I have learned much from anonymous cadres. There are the people of the encounters—citizens, officers, and observers whose identity was cloaked by warranty. There are the many officers of the staff and line who shared their reports prepared only for internal consumption. And there are those whose thoughts now are only mine. I owe much, too, to my many students and colleagues at the Center for Research on Social Organization at the University of Michigan. The closely knit corps of coworkers, Donald Dickson, Alan Levett, John Maniha, Maureen Mileski, and Jeff Piker, and collaborators, Howard Aldrich and Donald J. Black, are separately and collectively acknowledged for their contributions. Were I more responsible, I could point to the wisdom and assistance gained from my sometime colleague and collaborator, David Bordua, and my friends and perceptive critics Beverly Duncan, Dudley Duncan, G. Franklin Edwards, Lloyd Ohlin, and Paul Siegel. In recent years, the Friday fellowship of the law faculty at the University of Michigan provided many opportunities to profit from the continuing courtship between sociologists and lawyers. Colloquy with Frances Allen, Alfred Conard, Roger Cramton, Yale Kamisar, and Richard Lempert were especially stimulating.

My labor in writing was borne again and again by what must be the greatest fidelity and skill with typing assistance from the McEndarfer sisters, Judy and Sharon, Jane Hikel, and Margaret Bertsch. Mrs. Jane Isay and Mrs. Barbara MacAdam of the Yale University Press not only lightened my style but eased the pain of delivery.

I

A POLICEMAN'S LOT

Local police departments in the United States are part of an organized legal system of criminal justice and part of an organized community. Fundamentally, the police mediate between the community and the legal system. The police are the major representatives of the legal system in their transactions with citizens. They are responsible for enforcing all criminal laws, regardless of the willingness of the citizenry to be policed. Given their small numbers relative to the magnitude of their task, the police regard themselves as the "thin blue line" maintaining law and order in the community.

At the same time that the police enforce the law and keep the peace, they adapt the universal standards of the law to the requirements of citizens and public officials in the community. They do this primarily through their right to exercise discretion in determining whether or not violations of the law have taken place and whether citizens shall be arrested and charged with particular criminal offenses. Moreover, the police department, as an organization, adapts itself to meeting the demands of citizens for them to provide a variety of services, some unrelated to their law-enforcement role. They do so because they are the major emergency arm of the community in times of personal and public crisis.

Maintaining the Legitimacy of Police Authority
in Encounters

At law, the police in modern democratic societies such as the United States possess a virtual monopoly of the *legitimate* use of force over civilians.[1] Their legitimate right to intervene in the affairs of citizens, to enforce the law and keep the peace, also is unquestioned, provided it is done in legal ways. This monopoly and right to intervention in the affairs of citizens create a number of problems for the society. The principal problems involve maintaining the political neutrality of the police, the use of legal means in police behavior toward citizens, and the assurance that the police will use universal criteria in their discretion to apply the law.

The capacity of the police to maintain legality in their relations with citizens depends to an important degree upon their ability to establish and maintain the legitimacy of their legal authority. This is particularly difficult in a country like the United States where strong institutionalized norms support both aggression and violence on the part of citizens as well as suspicion or hostility toward police intervention.

The legitimacy of police intervention rests in constitutional law and in substantive and procedural law. In recent times much of the controversy over the legitimacy of police intervention has rested in the legality of means as defined in procedural law. Restrictions on search and seizure, interrogation, and privacy, for example, define what constitutes the legitimate use of police authority. Such definitions affect the organization of work within police departments.

A police organization also is confronted with public defi-

1. David J. Bordua and Albert J. Reiss, Jr., "Command, Control, and Charisma: Reflections on Police Bureaucracy," *The American Journal of Sociology* 72 (July 1966): 68–70; Albert J. Reiss, Jr., and David J. Bordua, "Organization and Environment: A Perspective on the Police," in David J. Bordua, ed., *The Police: Six Sociological Essays* (New York: John Wiley, 1967), pp. 28–40.

nitions of the legitimacy of intervention, some of which contravene the organization's legal rights. Illustrations of this disparity between legal and public definitions are evident in the 1960s in such areas as the enforcement of traffic laws and the handling of civil disorders. For example, although they are legal, many Americans object to unmarked police cars and traffic arrests by officers out of uniform. Similarly, command decisions to use plainclothesmen as well as uniformed police to make arrests in situations of public disorder are open to public debate. This practice was challenged when the New York City Police Department used plainclothes detectives to police student disorders on the Columbia University campus.

Nowhere in law enforcement is the problem of establishing legitimacy of authority more difficult, however, than in the day-to-day work of line officers in patrol. An examination of the work role of the patrol officer makes this abundantly clear.

The Work of Patrol

Patrol work usually begins when a patrolman moves onto a social stage with an unknown cast of characters. The settings, members of the cast, and the plot are never quite the same from one time to the next. Yet the patrolman must be prepared to act in all of them.

No other professional operates in a comparable setting. The bureaucratization and professionalization of work ordinarily eliminates this necessity by bringing clients to an office, a clinic, a hospital, or other bureaucratic setting where the client is "not at home." The physician's house call is almost a thing of the past. Now, the patient is usually processed by semiprofessionals, clerks, and technicians before the physician sees him. Even social workers have made considerable strides toward bringing clients into offices. So much so, that today the most progressive social-work programs are billed as "detached worker" programs, or "reaching out to the unreachables," where the social worker goes out to the client. Thus, it comes as no surprise that the newer poverty and economic opportunity programs, staffed largely by local community persons, soon succumb to the tenets of bureaucratization and professionalism. The clients are moved to neighborhood or community centers for processing. Even the police, in extending services through community relations programs, end up by opening a neighborhood office for clients. A "walk-in" service, however, usually begins with clients accepting the legitimacy of the enterprise and its personnel. Indeed, the service is designed to serve only those who do.

Patrolmen in a modernized police department are organized around a centralized command where men in cars are dispatched in response to citizen complaints received by telephone. This type of organization sharply contrasts with the traditional department where the foot patrolman (beat officer) moved in a limited territory on foot, knew his turf, and recognized the resident company of actors. Modern patrolmen must move continually from "stage" to "stage" in response to commands from general dispatchers, simply stating: "family trouble," "prowler," "disturbance," "boys in the street," or a "B & E" (breaking and entering). The scenery, the plot, and the actors may change dramatically in the course of a tour of duty.

The central command assigns patrolmen to a precinct commander who in turn assigns them to work in a particular territory or beat. To respond to central commands, each officer assumes the identity of his precinct and beat. He becomes, for instance, a 6–3 or a 9–4. Nominally, the officers on a particular beat are responsible for preventing crimes on their beat and responding to all calls for service within it. In practice, patrolmen are dispatched across the beats of a precinct, and if the beat is located at the perimeter of the precinct, they may be dispatched to another as well. The boundaries of a centralized command and communications system are governed by "who is available for dispatch," not who knows what about an area. The local precinct command tends also to downgrade specific knowledge in assigning patrol in modern departments. Responsive to an almost daily short roster because of furloughs, sick leaves, assignment to special duty, or less than a full complement, precinct captains resort to doubling of beats and reassignment based on prescriptions about generalists rather than specialists. More recently, the implementation of policies for the racial integration of cars on beat patrol has led to frequent rotation of at least some men, particularly those white officers most willing to serve with black officers.

The extent to which men are shifted from beat to beat and from partner to partner is apparent from the assignment of officers in the eight high-crime-rate precincts in Boston, Chicago, and Washington, D.C. Almost daily or weekly rotation of beat assignment was reported by 32 percent of all white and 29 percent of all Negro officers. An additional 14 percent of all white and 16 percent of all Negro officers had spent less than six months on the beat to which they were assigned. The older institution of partners who work closely together on a beat or assignment also appears to be passing; 51 percent of the white and 46 percent of the Negro officers were not assigned regularly with a partner in these precincts, owing partly, in Chicago and Washington, to the racial integration of scout cars. Another 15 percent of the white and 17 percent of the Negro officers had spent less than a month with the partner they had at the time of the observation study. Two-thirds of all the officers, then, were in unstable partner relationships. Knowledge of specific territory and a working partner relationship, while part of the ethos of police work, are hardly operating principles in high-crime-rate precincts.

Even when officers are engaged in preventive patrol responding to their own radar, their sensing devices are generally geared to automobiles; license numbers (hot cars), trouble spots, and suspicious persons or situations. At most, the patrol officer has specific knowledge of places he has been, trouble spots, a few known persons, the best places to pick up "movers" (moving traffic violations), and where the action is in ghetto areas (where the syndicate operates or where one can get most anything). Experience, which cannot be taught in police academies, serves as a guide to situations, plots, and actors. The patrolman comes to know when he is in potential danger even though in practice he may often ignore the signals. He learns to recognize—although, not without error—when a situation demands a quick response, when it is routine, and when, if he is slow to respond, the situation may resolve itself without police intervention.

The order of priority officers gave to dispatched mobilizations was examined in our observational studies of citizen mobilizations of the patrol. Of 4,371 dispatched encounters, the police evaluated 18 percent as requiring an urgent response. They drove rapidly to the scene of the dispatch, often using the flasher or siren to indicate the extreme urgency with which they regarded the dispatch for assistance. However, they treated 73 percent of all dispatches as clearly routine, observing all traffic rules and laws on the way to the scene, even, looking for a reasonable parking space. Six percent of all dispatches were considered so unimportant that police deliberately wasted time in approaching the scene of the dispatch: "It'll probably turn out to be nothing"; "no need to rush"; "we'll never catch him"; "if we go slow, that'll be over before we get there". What is more, in another 2 percent of all dispatches, they treated the matter as lower in priority than some other matter. Half of these higher priorities were purely personal; stopping to buy a pack of cigarettes or pick up dry cleaning, or even selling tickets to the policeman's benefit. For one dispatch in Detroit one evening, we drove to an officer's home more than four miles out of our way to pick up a dog the officer wanted to take to the veterinarian to be "put to sleep so the kids wouldn't know." During the next dispatch we drove more than six miles out of the way to leave the dog with the veterinarian. On the other hand, in about 50 percent of situations, higher priority was given to other police business, such as writing a traffic ticket for a moving violation (usually to fill one's ticket quota) or stopping to respond to the mobilization request of a citizen. In few such cases, of course, does the officer notify the central command that he has shifted priorities.

The social settings or stages where officers will work vary, of course, according to the social composition of the beat. Though the sizes of precincts and beats change with time as does the structure of communities, an officer's operating territory is generally quite variable. He moves across the class structure to a surprising degree, and from commercial to residential, or from "quiet" to "fast" action. A day's work for an officer does not necessarily provide diversity in action, but the weeks and months do. What is a crisis for the citizen and diversion for the outsider, becomes routine for the patrolmen. As already noted, in almost three-fourths of all dispatches, the patrolman moves to the scene in a routine fashion.

The settings in which encounters between the police and citizens takes place are as varied as the locations in any community. Clearly some settings are more common than others for particular types of offenses. To cite the obvious, most traffic violations occur on public streets, particularly moving violations, even though some standing violations occur on private property. As Stinchcombe shows, patterns of offenses known to the police are generally related to institutions of privacy in American society—the degree to which police can penetrate private places.[2] Citizen initiative in

2. Arthur Stinchcombe, "Institutions of Privacy in the Determination of Police Administrative Practice," *The American Journal of Sociology* 69 (September 1963): 150–60.

calling the police—the complaint—is the major legitimate avenue of the police to private places.

Unfortunately no official statistics are kept for the mobilization of the police to locations for all types of complaints or for offenses known to the police. The information in table 1.1 for selected offenses in Seattle, Washington shows the most common setting is the private dwelling (37 percent of all locations), followed by open places (29 percent), and commercial houses (24 percent). Relative to all Seattle locations, commercial houses are overrepresented in these mobilizations of the police.

While the type of crime varies considerably by location, a quick examination of locations to which officers are mobilized will also show that, for any given location such as a street, a business, or a dwelling unit, there is an extremely high probability that an officer, upon arrival, will be confronted by such *routine* matters as offenses against property; larceny, burglary, or destruction of property. In officers' language, such crimes are "cold." The burglary is not in progress; all the patrolman can do is take a report and turn it over to the detectives for investigation. If arrests are eventually to be made, they will be made by the investigating detectives, or the patrolman may later pick up the offender in some other crime situation.

Similarly, for offenses against the person, information is often general rather than specific. An officer only has cues to work by, such as "disturbance at," "family trouble," or "see a woman at." Even given specific information such as "man with a gun" or "robbery in progress," the scene is far from complete. The basic problem here is that the processing of information depends on relatively limited forms of communication. A citizen telephones the department and an officer must determine whether the situation warrants his making a discretionary decision to dispatch a car. However, the quantity and quality of the information obtained depends on many factors: the skill of the officer in seeking

Table 1.1

Percentage Distributions for Offenses Reported to the Police by Type of Location for Offense: Selected Offenses for Seattle, Washington, 1965

Location of incident	Homicide	Rape and attempt to rape	Robbery	Aggravated assault	Simple assault	Theft from person	Other larcenies	Burglary	Arson	Destruction of property	Total percentage	Total number
	Percentage of offenses reported for each type of location											
Open places (streets, etc.)	*	*	4	2	6	2	69	—	*	17	100	6,495
Offices	—	—	2	*	2	—	26	61	—	9	100	675
Commercial houses	*	*	2	1	3	1	54	31	*	8	100	5,311
Public buildings	*	*	1	1	7	1	79	4	*	6	99	776
Semipublic buildings	*	—	*	*	2	*	50	26	1	19	98	876
Dwelling units	*	1	1	2	9	*	43	31	1	12	100	8,134
Total percentage	*	*	2	2	6	1	54	21	*	13	99	—
Total number	24	85	473	374	1,395	231	12,031	4,755	96	2,803	—	22,267

Table 1.1—Continued

Location of incident	Homicide	Rape and attempt to rape	Robbery	Aggravated assault	Simple assault	Theft from person	Other larcenies	Burglary	Arson	Destruction of property	Total percentage
	Percentage of locations for each type of offense reported										
Open places (streets, etc.)	12	22	53	29	30	55	37	—	16	39	29
Offices	—	—	2	*	1	—	1	9	—	2	3
Commercial houses	17	13	28	16	12	24	24	33	9	15	24
Public buildings	8	2	2	2	4	5	5	*	2	2	3
Semipublic buildings	4	—	*	1	1	1	4	5	10	6	4
Dwelling units	59	63	15	52	52	15	29	53	63	36	37
Total percentage	100	100	100	100	100	100	100	100	100	100	100

*Less than 0.5 percent

and obtaining information, the amount of time he can spend getting the information, the emotional state of the citizen and his linguistic skills in providing information. In other words, the information an officer must act upon may not only be sketchy, but also misleading.

Our observational studies of police activity in high-crime-rate areas of three cities show that 87 percent of all patrol mobilizations were initiated by citizens. Officers initiated (both in the field and on view) only 13 percent. Thus, it becomes apparent that citizens exercise considerable control over police patrol work through their discretionary decisions to call the police. This is very important in terms of the legitimacy of police authority. When police enter a social setting, it is usually based on the assumption that at least one citizen believes the police have both a legitimate right and an obligation to enter that situation. This does not mean that the citizen mobilizer is always present in the situation to which the officer is called, but it does mean that almost nine out of ten times, the patrol officer enters a situation on citizen initiative.

The telephone is the principal means of communication whereby citizens mobilize the police; it is readily available to most citizens and is the fastest way of exchanging information. Of the 87 percent of police mobilizations initiated by citizens, 87 percent originated with a telephone call, 6 percent through citizen contact with the police at work in the field (e.g., flagging down a scout car), and 7 percent with walk-ins at precinct stations or headquarters. We examined all calls (some 4,000) received at the central communications center of the Chicago Police Department on June 20, 1965, in an effort to determine the content of the information system that originates with a citizen telephone call to the communications center of modern police departments. Table 1.2 shows the results based on calls to the Town Hall and Fillmore precincts. The information summarized is that which was available to the dispatcher and was usually com-

Table 1.2

Citizen Calls to Communications Center of Chicago Police
Department on June 20, 1965, by Mobilization Location:
Town Hall and Fillmore Precincts

Mobilization location designated by citizen's call	Town Hall	Fillmore	Total
Callers dwelling or premises	19	20	19
Callers building but not his dwelling	7	7	7
Dwelling unit of person other than caller	1	1	1
Street or block near caller	38	48	44
Commercial or quasi-public place near caller	18	16	17
Medical setting	6	2	4
Public places at distance from caller, e.g., while driving past	11	6	8
Total percentage	100	100	100
Total number	262	366	628

municated to the patrolmen in the scout car dispatched to the location of the incident.

The dispatcher possesses somewhat more information about location than he communicates. For example, he knows that some dispatches to a residential unit in table 1.2 are to a complainant's own residence while others are not. Nineteen percent of all calls concerned the caller's own dwelling units or premises, but 7 percent were complaints about some other unit within his building and 1 percent was for some other dwelling unit. These calls, 27 percent of all calls, were usually simply dispatches to a residential address so far as the patrolman was concerned. Often, the patrolman does not even know whether the complainant will be present when he arrives. The modal call for June 20 reported an incident in a street or block near the caller, a type of incident common during the summer season. However, in some of these situations, the transactions ultimately transpired within a dwelling unit, since the action moved there before, at the time of, or following the arrival of the scout car. Another 17 percent of calls originated from businesses or quasi-public places such as schools, 4 percent from medical settings, and 8 percent in special street locations such as those of automobile accidents. In 7 percent of all calls, the dispatcher only secured an address, thereby leaving the officer with the minimum amount of information. To be sure, even when the dispatcher possesses information on the type of location, he may not communicate it to patrol. That often lies within his discretion and a dispatch stating the general nature of an incident and the address is considered sufficient.

A communications center screens calls, so that dispatches will not be sent out in all instances. For all dispatches the center operates on the presumption that the information is, in all probability, valid. However, experience indicates that this is not always the case. The Chicago Police Department has found that a substantial proportion of anonymous calls turn out to be fruitless; yet the payoff on many anonymous tips or calls is sufficient in official judgment to warrant investigation. Other reasons why calls may not actually be investigated include matters ranging from errors in communication to situations that change before the police arrive.

Of the dispatches to mobile patrol where one of our observers was present, 30 percent of the citizen initiated incidents led to no police-citizen interaction whatsoever. In many such dispatches it was as difficult for our observers to understand why this was so as it was for the police. Most of these, however, were not criminal incidents, at least as defined by the original dispatch. They included situations in which it was unlikely that a citizen would be present: ringing burglar alarms, parking violations, abandoned cars, and suspicious situations (a car parked with the motor running).

Other cases in which the citizens who made the complaint as well as the citizens reported as offending could not be expected to be present when the police arrived include suspicious persons, or rowdy boys in the street and other noise disturbances in all of which the caller may have already scared off the offenders by threatening to call the police. Still other calls may hinge on unfounded presumptions: calls about prowlers (who may never have been there), or shootings that may not have occurred, or a suspected fire.

For many such cases, when the police arrive and see no one, they may only take a quick look around and leave. When police officers are dispatched to situations where there are no citizens to offer guidelines for action, they do very little. For 1 in 5 such incidents, they do almost nothing, even though our observers thought some investigation could have been undertaken. The officers could have gotten out of the car and looked around, for example, but they did not.

To understand this, one must bear in mind that, for policemen, police work is, after all, work. Much that police officers do not do on their routine tour of duty can be easily explained by simple platitude. Like all jobs, police work includes restriction of output and avoidance of work that cannot be easily assessed or observed. Police, not unlike factory workers, as Collins, Dalton, and Roy, among others, have consistently noted,[3] avoid work as well as do work.

A sizeable proportion of citizen mobilizations of the police are to public places, such as streets, and to quasi-public places, such as businesses and schools (as the data in tables 1.1 and 1.2 show). However, our observations of citizen initiated encounters in eight high-crime-rate areas of Boston, Chicago, and Washington, D.C., indicate that a much higher proportion of calls investigated occur in private places, where citizens are more likely to be present, than in public or semipublic places:

3. Orville Collins, Melville Dalton, and Donald Roy, "Restriction of Output and Social Cleavage in Industry," *Applied Anthropology* 5 (Summer 1946): 1–14.

Specific Setting of Encounter	*Percentage of All Encounters*
Enclosed private place: within dwelling	36
Open private place: porch, yard, premises	34
Semiprivate place: within business	7
Semiprivate place: all other	5
Open public place	18

Indeed, 70 percent of citizen initiated encounters, where a citizen was present when the police arrived, occurred within or about a private place.[4]

One reason for this is that in citizen calls about public places, complainants, or other citizens are less likely to be around when the police arrive than they are in calls about private places. But, there is also a difference in the nature of calls for service in high-crime-rate areas. Despite the high rate of crimes against persons in public places and against businesses in these areas, such crimes comprise less than one-third of all police business in ghetto areas. Citizens in high-crime-rate areas mobilize the police for a large variety of services—sick calls, domestic crises, and disputes of all kinds. The police will not treat most of these calls as criminal matters.

As table 1.3 shows, within high-crime-rate areas, a majority of all incidents, other than traffic, took place within or near private places. And, no more than about one-fifth of any type of encounter, other than those involving complaints, took place in an open public setting. Not unexpectedly, however, noncriminal disputes, more than any other type of incident, were mediated or arbitrated in private rather than public places. Even felonies and misdemeanors were primarily breaches of private order. Quite clearly, in

4. See Donald J. Black, "Police Encounters and Social Organization: An Observation Study" (Ph.D. diss., University of Michigan, 1968), chaps. 2 and 3.

Table 1.3

Percentage of Citizen Initiated Encounters According to the General Type of Incident, by Specific Setting of Encounter

Specific setting of encounter	General type of incident									
	Felony	Misde-meanor	Traffic viola-tion	Juve-nile trou-ble	Suspi-cious person or sit-uation	Non-crimi-nal dis-pute	Service	Unfounded	Other	All inci-dents
Enclosed private place: within dwelling	43	35	6	16	38	55	37	27	47	36
Open private place: porch, yard, etc.	27	33	37	53	37	31	35	34	23	34
Semipublic place: within business	8	10	1	6	7	7	3	14	9	7
Semipublic place: other	5	4	4	3	1	*	10	3	2	5
Open public place	17	18	52	22	16	7	14	21	19	18
Total percentage	100	100	100	100	99	100	99	99	100	100
Total number	(554)	(637)	(154)	(346)	(73)	(467)	(553)	(157)	(47)	(2,988)

*0.5 percent or less

the lowest socio-economic areas, citizens get in touch with and have contact with the police primarily about problems that arise within or near their households. Police dealings with lower socio-economic groups involve, for the most part, preserving the integrity of private order.

Police officers must be prepared to deal with varying numbers of people in these different social settings. There may be large numbers in picket lines, sit-ins, unruly crowds or mob, drivers in traffic, or audiences at mass events. Though superficially their role is to preserve the peace by coping with any individuals in the large aggregation who violate laws, they must be prepared to restore order as well. The major work emphasis in such settings is on team work, and, in restoring or maintaining public order, their work is generally paramilitary.

Most of the time, however, officers in patrol work are in two-man teams or alone. They must be prepared to work primarily with more than one individual, particularly in high-crime-rate areas of our larger cities. In only one-fourth of police patrol encounters in table 1.4 were the police dealing with a single citizen. The modal police encounter includes more citizens than officers. Assuming, typically, one or two officers in a police encounter with citizens, 54 percent of the observed encounters included three or more citizens and 27 percent, five or more.

Comparing police encounters in high-crime-rate Negro areas with those in white areas, encounters with white citizens were more likely to include a smaller number of citizens. While 30 percent of all encounters with whites were with a lone citizen, a lone Negro citizen was encountered in only 23 percent of patrol mobilizations. Five or more Negro citizens were present in 28 percent of police encounters with Negroes as compared with 21 percent of those for whites. Officers in predominantly Negro areas then are faced with potentially greater problems of control solely by reason of larger number of citizens.

Table 1.4

Percentage Distribution by Number of Citizens Present in Encounters with the Police, by Race of Citizen and Type of Mobilization of the Police

Race of citizen*	Type of mobilization	Total number of encounters	Total percentage	Number of citizens in encounter (as percentage of total)				
				1	2	3	4	5 or more
White and Negro†	Dispatch	3,010	100	22	22	16	12	28
	On-view	614	100	38	20	14	7	21
	Citizen-in-field	202	100	27	22	20	9	22
	All mobilizations	3,826	100	25	21	16	11	27
White	Dispatch	1,351	100	27	24	16	11	22
	On-view	262	100	44	22	12	7	15
	Citizen-in-field	104	100	32	25	19	6	18
	All-white	1,717	100	30	24	15	10	21
Negro	Dispatch	1,540	100	20	22	16	13	29
	On-view	315	100	39	17	16	6	22
	Citizen-in-field	89	100	20	20	19	16	25
	All-Negro	1,944	100	23	21	16	12	28

*Race data are lacking for 165 encounters.
†Excluded are 43 encounters where both white and Negro citizens were present as participants (excluding by-standers).

Police officers must deal not only with the actors on stage, but often with an audience as well. This audience may be comprised of members of a family, strangers in the street, or a mob. The officers must assess the audience as well as the actors, since the audience may have an important effect on police work. Are the members cooperative or hostile? Can they supply information? How can they be utilized in the situation? The police must be concerned with the audience's acceptance of them as well as with their own judgment and control of that audience.

For our studies, we have chosen five major types of citizen roles that participate in police situations. The principal actors are generally complainants, suspects, and offenders. Minor roles may be played by informants about the central participants, the action, or the situation, or by observer-bystanders, who can shift to more active participatory roles as situations change. For dispatched encounters, citizens stand as the major complainants; in on-view encounters, officers fulfill this role. Many dispatches include only complainants, as when the police are called about crimes that have already occurred. When a situation is in progress at the time the officers arrive, it is fairly likely it will include complainants and suspects or offenders. Of the 72 percent of all encounters that included citizens, offenders or suspects were present in 39 percent.

This characterization of the social stages, the participants, and even of the action for all police work in an area fails to capture the shifts that may occur for a policeman in his tour of duty. No tour of duty is typical except in the sense that *the modal tour of duty does not involve an arrest* of any person, and traffic citations may be written on many such tours depending upon whether or not the department has a quota system of ticket citations for patrol. This is not to say that arrests could not have been made on many tours of duty, but often they are not because the officer exercises his discretion not to make such arrests.

Even when tours of duty include the arrest of one or more persons, it is usually for misdemeanors such as drunkenness or disorderly conduct rather than for felonies. Consider the following summary of an observer's account of an 11 P.M.–7:30 A.M. tour of duty during July 1965 in Chicago's predominantly Negro Fillmore area (familiar as the scene of two major riots in 1965 and 1966).

At 11:50 P.M., the two white officers were dispatched to "a disturbance." They were met on the landing of an apartment house, and the action took place there and in the apartment. A Negro female was the central complainant and the offenders, whom she charged with infidelity, were her husband and a woman. The officers "sweet talked" the woman into leaving, temporarily restoring order to the household, and they left at 12:40 A.M. A few minutes later they were dispatched to an apartment on a complaint of loud music disturbing the tenants. The complainant was nowhere visible and a knock at an apartment with blaring music brought forth one young Negro woman and her four male friends. On being told to turn down the music, one of the Negro males became quite vocal, asking: "Why are you whiteys always coming into colored neighborhoods and telling us what to do?" Some further talk brought the music down and the officers left just after 1 A.M. As they drove about the beat, at 1:47 A.M. they were flagged down by two Negro males who stated someone had been trying to steal their car. Inspection disclosed possible tampering with the car. The officers said they would make a report and that the detectives would follow it up. They returned to their car at 2:05 A.M. At 2:25, they were given a run to an unspecific disturbance. They arrived and were met by a Negro woman on a porch who complained about a white drunk in her house. When the officers got inside, the drunk had made it to the porch where he passed out. The officers regarded the woman as a "regular," known as "Angel." They called the wagon to take the man in. When the wagon crew arrived and a finger lock failed to revive him so he might walk to the wagon, one of the wagon officers went to the wagon, returned, and doused the drunk with ammonia. His painful outcry was instantaneous and he was led in blind rage and outcries to the wagon. One of the dispatched officers mused that "Angel" made a dirty business off white men whom she got drunk, and then called the wagon to take them away. Shortly after their return to the car they were driving to lunch when a citizen flagged them down. He was a trucker who wanted them to provide surveillance while he unloaded a truck at the rear of an A & P store. The officers slyly commented to one another that there would be some material reward and went willingly. Their willingness soon turned to disappointment when they discovered it was only a bread truck, but they complied.

Following a break for lunch, they were given a call for another disturbance, one involving a boyfriend. On arrival, it turned out that the complainant sought protection from anticipated consequences. She had been out with another man; her boyfriend had found out, and she anticipated he would beat her up when he came in. The officers talked with her, advising her to lock the door and call the police if he tried to get in. With that they left at 4:11 A.M. Except for a brief call to escort another car, a standby matter, the tour was spent in riding and small talk until 7:30 when they returned to the station.

Of such evenings is much police work made.

A night in Detroit's 10th precinct, a predominantly Negro area, was reported by an observer who rode the 4 P.M. to midnight tour of duty.

The observer joined the two white officers, Chet and Bob, when they came into the station bringing in a Negro man on traffic warrants. Bob had been on the force and in this precinct for ten years and was the "number two" man of his beat car. Chet had been on the force less than a year and it was his first night on with Bob; as yet he had no regular assignment.

As soon as the officers did the minimum paper work, the man was informed he could get out on a $25 bond after clearance of his prints. We took off, since they had another run.

The run was to meet a woman at a phone booth about family trouble. As we drove, I was asked my usual bit about what I was interested in and gave my usual reply about comparing problems in police departments and how the organization met them, emphasizing the organization. I said that one of the best ways to know what is going on is to be with the men who are on the line and see their problems. My experience is that men in supervisory positions have been out of the line so long they no longer know the problems. This almost invariably brings a positive response from the men. It did here too.

Bob began: "You're right. The men downtown just don't know what's going on around here. Take like now they are telling us that we have the highest traffic accident rate of any district in the city. They look at how many tickets we write out here and see that we don't write as many tickets as some areas. They get after us then to write more tickets. What they don't see, at the same time, is that we are the busiest district in the whole city, that we are kept busy on things other than traffic. We don't have the time to go out and get tickets. We run all night just keeping up with the runs in our area. The trouble with them is they just look at the one thing—not what we have to do. They also think that all you have to do is look and you can find a violator. Well it's easy to get that idea. They see them all the time driving into work and so do I, but it's another thing to just sit at corners or move around to catch violators. You don't get them that way. I see fewer of them when I'm at work than when I just drive around off duty. Last week when they began the traffic-enforcement week, they put the pressure on this district. So, beginning on

Monday, the pressure was on to increase the number of tickets in this district. They even sent about twenty-five motorcycles from other areas into this one. Well, do you know that the first night we looked like everything—we had more time since it was a Monday night—but we didn't find a single mover. I mean, not a single one, and we really looked. You can always find a borderline parker who is a foot or two out of his area, but we don't go for stuff like that. That's not a legitimate traffic violation and we won't write it up."

We got to the corner and saw the phone booth but no one was there. So we sat at the corner a few minutes to wait. Bob asked me what I thought of the Civil Review Boards. Had I seen the one in Philadelphia. I told him that in general I thought the problem was more one of how you dealt with the matter than the boards themselves and that I thought the boards had many dangers in them so far as the development of a professionalized police force was concerned. He responded: "Well we got the biggest Civil Review Board in this city right now. It's called the Community Relations Bureau. All they do is apply pressure on the police and make claims about what we are and aren't doing." I mistook it for the CRB in the PD for a moment and cautiously asked who ran it and was responsible for it. He replied by saying he didn't know but they were a big pressure group coming into the districts. I recognized that he was talking about block clubs, etc., and then asked him how about the one downtown. He said, "Well that's staffed by police officers, but you would never know it. They act like they were against us. They will accept anyone's word against the police." I asked him, "Do you know of any specific cases where they did that?" He said, "Well, there was a guy on the force and this colored family moved in next door to him. I'm not saying that he was happy about it; he wasn't, but he knew there was nothing to do. Well he had this dog and they complained about it and he told them it was his dog and there wasn't a damn thing they could do about it. So they complained to the Commu-

nity Relations Bureau and they called him in and wanted to
know what he was doing insulting the citizen. Then about
two weeks later the colored family's house was set on fire and
the first thing they did was to walk into this officer's house
and try to accuse him of setting it. Now, I ask you doesn't an
officer have any rights in his own home?" I said I thought he
had the usual citizen's rights. He replied, "Well we know he
doesn't, even though we'd like to think so. That's what you
get out of the Community Relations Bureau though—they'll
accept anyone's word over that of an officer; they don't follow police investigation routines."

By this time, it was clear no one was going to show up to
claim they wanted help in a family trouble situation, so we
moved down the block to the call box to make a report. Since
there was no run, we moved around the corner and on down
to 12th Street, the busy street of the area according to the
officers and also according to the wall map in the station. I
noted before we came out that the wall map showed several
purse snatchings, eight B & Es, three assaults, and other offenses on this street for the first ten days of October. There
were two rapes just off the street. Prostitution also is heavy.
There are houses of prostitution, blind pigs, numbers oper-
ators, etc. on Twelfth Street. It is the heaviest scout car area
of the district.

We weren't a block into Twelfth Street when a Negro man
hailed us down and Bob rolled down the window (Chet was
driving the first four hours). The man began by saying he
wanted to go downtown and he wanted a ride. Bob said they
weren't a taxi service, so he should get a taxi. The man (44
years of age) said that he owed $35 for traffic tickets and that
he wanted to go downtown. Bob told him that he'd have to
get down there by himself and pay them. The man persisted
and said that he didn't have the money and Bob said, "Oh,
you want me to arrest you," and the man said "Yes." So he
said, "get in," and the man did. There followed a lot of shuf-
fling through papers to get the ticket notices; the man wanted

to know about how he could get the matter cleared up so he could get his license from Lansing, and so on. Bob looked it all over and then turned around to talk to the man, who sat next to me. He began, "Now let me tell you just what is going to happen to you. We're going to take you into our station and book you on this. Now then, you'll spend the weekend in the lockup and on Monday morning you'll go to Judge Wood's court. Now the way Judge Wood usually handles this is if you spend Saturday night and Sunday in the lockup and come to court on Monday, he'll count that three days if you sit out the court session on Monday and that will take care of your $35, so you won't owe anything on these. If you go out on bond, you'll still have to pay the tickets on Monday." The man said he had no money and he'd just go to sleep. "I would like to go to work on Monday. My boss gave me the money." Bob asked, "What happened, did you lose it all on her?" And joking, he said, "What was she like?" The man laughed—"Her name was Alice and she was some horse. She took me for all of it and now I can't go back and tell my boss I lost it, so this is the way I can get it cleared up if I can get to work on Monday." A few minutes later he said, "Well, he may come get me out and I'll tell him I needed the money in jail for cigarettes and things like that and then my credit will be good and maybe next time if I want $40 he'll give it to me." There was some joshing about this. Bob went on to explain, "Now when you get your tickets straightened out, then go upstairs and have them give you a form to send to Lansing, telling them you are OK on your fines and then you can get your license. OK?" The man nodded OK.

We went back to talking about bird dogs, a conversation dear to Bob's heart and one he had just begun before the man hailed us. We took him around to the lockup at the station and he was booked by station personnel, so it took us only about five minutes.

As we came into the station, two officers pointed out a Cadillac in the garage with a lot of men's suits in the trunk.

It looked familiar. When we got in, I saw the big guy from my last sally into 10-4 was at the desk in back being booked. He was the guy who passed the money to the rider in the hit-and-run case, my last trip out. He was in now for having been stopped on a moving violation in an alley and when they checked they found traffic warrants on him. He was protesting being booked and having to put up a bond. The clothing still is unexplained—he claims to have $3,500 in merchandise in the trunk.

We left without a run. As we came out of the station lot, Bob spotted a mover—a foreign car without taillights. He told Chet, "Well there's our mover. Chet had just been turning right and the car was headed in the opposite direction. He was very proper and went to the intersection to make a U-turn and then follow. By this time there were four or five other cars in between the mover and us. We got through the light but he was held up by oncoming traffic. We finally saw the man turn into a store parking lot. Chet again waited for traffic and we lost the man in the lot. Bob finally said, "Well you aren't making things very easy for me. You learned something else new—if you are going to go after a mover, get after him right then and there—don't wait to go down and turn, turn then and follow even if you have to back around and hold up traffic. (I found out later that Chet had a traffic accident with a scout car two months ago and he may be overly cautious yet.) In any case, the car was gone. Bob told him to turn and go out of the lot. As we began to move out we heard a call for 14-12 to investigate a fight in the Sears lot behind the Victor Paint Store. That was right next to the lot we were in. Bob got out and said to me, "Come on, let's walk over there and look at that." He told Chet to meet us at the side of the paint store. We walked over to the lot within two or three minutes and could spot no fight. Bob finally walked over to a car in which a man was sitting and asked him if he had seen a fight. The man explained that he had been dozing and heard this noise and there was an older

*white man having an argument with a young colored man.
They were arguing about a parking space. They were starting
to swing at one another but he and some others went over
and told the young man to lay off the other guy as he was an
old man. The guy went off. He didn't know anyone had
turned in the alarm. He sort of kept talking, but Bob kept
moving away, telling him thanks a lot and glad he was able
to help in this case and we moved away from him. Just then
the Sears manager came up to us. He, too, was looking for it
and mumbled, he didn't realize they had been called. Bob
said nothing and we walked off. Chet wasn't at the side of the
paint store. The other scout car that got the run came up and
Bob told them there was nothing to it. He then asked if they'd
seen our car. They said no they hadn't but would put in a
call for it. Bob said, "No don't. We're 10 and this is 12. He'll
come back or we'll walk to the station."*

*They moved off. He said, "That's the thing with these new
guys. When you got one of them, it's like having one arm. I
don't see why it takes so long for them to pick things up. But
maybe I was like that too when I started out." I mentioned
that I knew Chet was new—Bob said, not more than two
months, he'd bet—(almost a year as I later discovered). Chet
finally came along, obviously after having executed all of the
correct traffic maneuvers. To Bob's where have you been, he
said he came into the lot from the other side and didn't see us.*

*He told Chet to go down the street, turn left, and go over
on X street. He had a run to meet a man at an apartment
house. I thought we were on our way to it, and when we
pulled up in front of a house, I started to get out after Bob.
Chet told me that wasn't the run and said nothing more. Bob
opened the trunk and went down the alley, he came back
with something and put it into the trunk. Then he told Chet
how to drive to the run street. A dog began to make noise in
back and he said to me, "You can tell she's not used to riding
back there." I asked him whether he was taking her to the
vets. He said yes and that his girl was going to be upset but*

he couldn't have this mutt around with the new dog. He had just acquired a new bird dog. He went on to say, "This was the bad one of the litter—funny how kids always pick that one out." On the way to the run he talked about how he had gotten taken on a bird dog last year.

We got to the apartment house and there was a white janitor waiting for us at the street. He told us that a man had been bothering the tenants and him by not moving out of the lobby. He pointed out that the man was going down the street. Bob asked if he was drunk and the man said yes. We moved down the street and the man was just at the corner as we got there. Bob told Chet to let him move across the street and we went and Bob called him over when he got across. The man was a tall colored man, obviously somewhat drunk. He finally produced identification showing that he was Daniel Thornton (a Canadian fishing license for Ontario Province). There was no driver's license or other identification so Bob thought he might be wanted on warrants. They questioned him about where he was going and he said home and gave his address. Bob pointed out that was in the opposite direction. The man indicated the usual drunk's confusion and started to argue. Bob told him to get in and we went to a call box where he was checked out for warrants. On the way to the box, Bob kept kidding him about his dangler's license. This confused the man further as he didn't know what Bob was referring to. Finally, he told him that he fished too. As Bob got out of the car the man launched into a drunk's talk about fishing and in between was how everyone was happy when they went fishing, etc. The mucous from his nose dripped into his mustache and he looked more and more like the drunk. Bob came back and told him he was clean. He then went back to why did he bother those people at the apartment house. The man said he didn't. Bob told him he must have because they complained. The man started to argue and Bob said, "Look, if you're going to argue, I'll take you on in; if you behave, I'll take you home." The man *laughed and withdrew and said, "That's it, take me home; that's what I want." He mumbled the usual inebriate's phrases as we took him to his address (Bob had told him before, it had a white porch, etc.—he knows every place in this very small scout car area—obviously). When we got there, the man started to argue again. Bob told him to get on in or they would run him in and that if they found him out again that night, they would run him in. The man said, yes, and we drove off without waiting to see if he went in.*

Bob told Chet to head toward Ford Hospital and cross Woodward, etc. We went to the vet's about four or five miles away and left the dog there. Chet told me that he had been on a year, that he thought the department was lowering standards. He had been in a class of only eleven where everyone had at least two years of college. He went on: "I don't think that any policeman should have less than two years of college and now they are taking them with only two years of high school. I don't think that is near enough; I had three years myself, and I think you need that. Under Edwards, they lowered it to two years of high school and some examination. I hear that they took some men from the department who met with those who applied—the colored applicants— and told them the answers to the examination questions and still a lot of them failed." At this point, Bob came out and we went on since we had a run for an illegal parking ticket.

We got to a home and saw no illegal parking. I went to the door with Bob, and a Negro woman—lower-middle-class type—answered the door and when Bob asked about the parking, she said: "Oh I called the station to tell them that he had moved his car. I saw him there in front of the driveway and knew my husband would be home soon, so I called to report it. Sorry." Bob said, "Oh they never cancel those since it might be the person parking, so we check them out anyway." She said, "Well, my husband is a plasterer and he'll be home soon and I wanted to be sure he could get in. Sorry to bother you." Bob said, "That's OK, hope he doesn't come home plastered." She said, "No, he'll just come home tired and dirty and clean up." He said, "Well, call us any time," and we left. I couldn't tell how much of this humor was simply his brand and how much was directed at the Negro as a target. I suspect more of the latter, but I had almost no opportunity to see him work with whites during the night. So, it's hard to say.

They called in and there was a run. Bob came back to the car from the box and said, "Well now you're going to have to do some police work. There's a four-year-old girl missing." We were at the place in two or three minutes, out of the car fast, and up on the porch. When we got inside, a well-dressed woman—black bourgeoisie, in Frazier's terms—came to the door and was soon joined by three teenagers (two boys and a girl) also well-dressed. She began by apologizing saying that the girl was now home. The girl came down the steps and ran to her mother. Bob said to the girl, "Did you run away because you wanted 4,000 policemen to look for you. You shouldn't do that, honey. I'll bet you wanted them to do that, didn't you?" She said, "I don't want to go to jail." He said, "You won't honey, but don't do that again. You scared your mother and you could really get lost. Don't do that again." The mother said, "She said some woman came and took her to the party after I told her she couldn't go. We were just across the street at a reception and she wasn't supposed to go out." Bob said, "Well, we're glad she's safe," and we turned to go. He said to the girl, "Bye, bye honey, now you be good" as we went out the door. This is part of his technique of treating Negroes, I think. He gets a good response with it, as one might expect with a good many, but I'm sure some may resent it.

As we left, he said, "Well I'm glad she's there. I have no desire to go looking for her tonight. Hope all of this so far isn't the way the night is going to go."

We went down the street and were about to go on when we saw a fight on the corner between four people. We got out and ran to the corner. An older Negro man and his wife were obviously aligned on one side and two girls (a dike and a bulldagger by Bob's statement later) were on the other. The main fight was between the dike and the woman. The woman was shrilling about, "You leave me alone" and "You've been put away and are on that dope; what for you push me around and was after her." The bulldagger was attempting to restrain the dike who was shouting: "You mother f————; you cocks———— sure I've been away, but I've got a better place than you, I'll bet; what makes you think you're so damn good. You mother f———— you," and on and on with the expletives. The man was looking for something and Chet started to talk to him while Bob tried to talk to the older, reasonably well-dressed Negro woman (the husband had a black suit with black tie). They were obviously going out "semiformal." She started to shrill that this woman attacked her as she came out of the store: "I don't know why; I don't know why; I don't even know her—just saw her around here until she was put away and now she's back. She just came up and after me." The dike shrilled back her profanity. Bob told the bulldagger to get her friend down the street or he would run her in. The dike looked a bit wild or high and had her hair done in flat curls on her face and distorted her features as she shrilled and resisted the bulldagger. Her bulldagger finally dragged her off by putting her arms behind her back and they went down the street, fighting as they went. Further inquiry from the woman brought the same story about her being unable to say why she was attacked as she came out of the store across the street. The man's finger was cut and he said that the dike had pulled a knife on them and when he went after it, she cut his finger. Bob asked him if he wanted to sign a complaint, and he said, "No, I'll settle things with her; I'll get her." With that, Bob started off back to the car. Chet got down on his hands and knees to find the knife and finally saw a paring knife under a car. He tried to get it, but since Bob already was back to the

car, he got up and went back to it. Bob's comment was
simple. "That dike and her bulldagger are looking for
trouble." That was it.

As we turned down Twelfth Street and were about to do
a little police work, as Bob calls it (the standard term, of
course), a woman, about forty-five came up and banged at
the window as we pulled to the curb. She was crying pro-
fusely and wiping her eyes. Bob asked her, "What's the matter?" She began her tale of woe, sobbing, wiping her eyes
with her handkerchief, and moaning. "I don't know what's
the matter; I've been beaten up. I just don't know. We were
going to be married tomorrow, we've got the marriage
license and had the blood test and everything and then
when I got home from work he just hit me. He hit me across
the mouth and on the head and here on my legs—he pushed
me down and look at my knees [shows them]. I don't know
if he's out of his head or what; he ain't never done this before. Ohoooo." Bob said, "Wait a minute now, is he drunk?"
She said, "Well, he's been drinking. But I don't know. He
must be out of his head or something, cause we were going
to get married and we had the license and the blood test and
all that. Oh, what can I do, that's my place and he hit me."
Bob said, "Do you want to sign a complaint against him and
we'll get him out?" She said, "Oh, I don't know what I want
to do. You know, we were going to be married and all that
and then I came home and he hits me and knocks me down;
I don't know what I want to do. He ain't never done that
before." Bob said, "Well, has he ever hit you before?" She
said, "Well just once." Bob said, "What did you do then?"
"Well, I didn't do anything. He hit me and I blacked out
and when I came to he was gone." Bob said, "How long
has he been living with you?" She said, "Well almost two
years, but we were going to be married." Bob said, "Maybe
he doesn't want to get married." She broke into more tears,
showed her missing front teeth as she sobbed and said, "No,
he had to wait that long for the divorce so we could get mar-

ried. And then he didn't have a job. I work at Mr. Hughes'
and he lived with me." Bob said, "Well if you don't want to
sign a complaint, why don't you go somewhere else tonight
and go back in the morning and tell him to get out. He'll
probably be sober then." She said, "I don't have any place
to go." He said, "Well why don't you go over to Mr. Hughes'
and tell him and call the guy up and tell him to get out."
She went on, "I can't let him know that he did this to me.
I've lived in this area for four years—I don't want to brag
and I've been good—I've got a good reputation, I raised two
children who are good, and Mr. Hughes is such a good man,
I just couldn't let him know that." She sounded so convincing.
Bob told her, "Well, why don't you go over to Mr. Hughes
and don't tell him anything. Have a cup of coffee and think
over what you want to do; then if you want to sign a complaint against him, call us and we'll take him in." She said,
"Oh, I don't want Mr. Hughes to know." He replied, "Well
go and have a cup of coffee, and think over what you want
to do and if you want to sign a complaint, call us." She
started back through the now familiar routine about the
license, the blood test, and he must be out of his head. Bob
again urged her to have a cup of coffee. By now her hankie
was sodden, so she took a white glove out of her purse and
dabbed her eyes. She finally turned from the car with Bob
exhorting her to think it over. As we drove away, Bob said,
"Imagine what he wants—he doesn't want to marry her and
he's getting rid of her. Mr. Hughes is such a nice man. He
runs a numbers game and that place is filled with prostitutes.
Bet that's her last chance to get married and he isn't going
to go through with it. If he met her at Mr. Hughes', imagine
what he was looking for. He had it soft for two years—that
divorce bit. And with that information, somehow my involvement wasn't quite the same." I saw the tragedy and
felt sorry for the woman, but the tragedy was set in the
dramatic terms of the lower class with the usual cast of
characters, including the police.

As we went down the street, we had a call for a run to an apartment where a woman was complaining about a man in the hall. We went to the apartment and a woman finally responded to the knocks with a "Who's there?" The response of the police finally brought an open door. There stood a short, fat, blind, Negro woman with the usual cane. She asked us to come in and we had difficulty crowding in past her. Her sight was largely gone. There was a mouse under her left eye where she had been hit and she pointed out the bruises on her legs. She began, "I want a peace bond for my husband. He won't leave me alone and drinks and beats me and follows me over here to aunty's. I've got a key to aunty's place and he knows it and comes over here. He beat me this way last night and started again tonight and I came over here. I want a peace bond on him." Bob said, "Well, you have to go downtown to get that. You could sign a complaint and we could take him into Livernois station tonight, but then he could get out and might only be fined. You want a peace bond, so you'll have to go downtown for that on Monday. This is Saturday and they're closed until Monday. You have to go to the prosecutor's for that." She said, "That's what I want, a peace bond so he'll leave me alone. See, he's in my place and I have to come over here to aunty's. My son lives here with her—he's not his father and when he gets that way, I come here." Bob asked her how long he's been that way. She said, "Well we've been married nine years and he's always beat me. I've been blind since 1958 and he's been getting worse. He says that the rehabilitation people are doing things with me—you know, not nice. Some of thems men and he says they are after me—well you know they aren't interested in that. They're interested in helping me, but he don't see that and he drinks and gets mad and accuses me and beats me." Bob said, "Well why don't you leave him." "I have—lots of times, but then he comes around and nice talks me and tells me he'll be different and I go back, but each time he's meaner. So this time I want a peace bond so *he won't bother me no more." Bob said, "Well does he support you?" She said, "Well he is supposed to give me $20 a week but when he lives with me he doesn't and then he says I should do the work and keep the place and you know I can't do that like this and then he beats me for it. That's why I want the peace bond—that'll keep him from beating me won't it?" Bob said, "Yes, the peace bond will tell him to let you alone. Now, I'll tell you what to do, you go down to 1000 Beaubien on Monday to the prosecutor's office and get a peace bond and then you go up on Warren off Woodward to the Legal Aid Society—there are lawyers there who give their time to help people like you—and you get their advice. You need a lawyer too, you probably need to get a divorce and make him support you. He's supporting you now, isn't he?" She said, "Well when he works, he is supposed to give me $20 a week, but I don't always get that and when he didn't work I got blind welfare of $80 for the month." Bob said she might get some additional welfare but that legal aid would help her. She finally repeated what he told her about what she should do and said she would stay at aunty's and go down and do that on Monday—"because what I want is a peace bond."*

After we left, Bob asked me about Chicago and did they have lots of Negro officers. I told him quite a few and that I had ridden with them. He said, "We used to have a Negro partner on this car. He was very bright and well-educated— quoted Darwin and all that and liked to discuss evolution. But we just couldn't have him on the car after a year or so. He was a party type—he would drink and go out with the women and then if we were on the late shift, he would sleep a lot of the time and miss the calls if we got out of the car or put all of the work on you if you were with him. It's not that he was a Negro, but he just wasn't a police officer. So we finally asked them to take him off." I asked where he was now and they said in a quieter area of the district and they guessed he was doing all right since it wasn't so busy there.

He asked me whether the number of Negro officers in Chicago was increasing and I said that it looked that way. He said, "Well it's fewer here now than it was a couple of years ago." I asked why. "Well they've had to let a lot go because they don't make good officers and not enough have come in. The people around here don't like Negro officers —they feel they've turned against them being of their own kind and the officers can't take that. We're used to it and besides we get along pretty well. This Negro guy who worked with us did too. He was OK at first until he became a party type."

Since we were going down Twelfth Street then, he pointed out Mr. Hughes' place to me. Just beyond, Chet and Bob saw a man with two women and Bob said, "Isn't that the guy in the picture?" Chet pulled it down and said that it looked like him so they called him over for a better look. Bob asked him his name and then decided he wasn't the guy and said to him, "We are just checking—thought we had your picture here but it's not you." The guy laughed nervously and said, "they didn't have no picture of him, he'd bet." We drove off. We talked about ambulance runs and Bob said, "We used to do a lot of sick-call runs. But not any more. We spent most of our time on that some nights. And we couldn't handle our regular runs. So out here we just quit." I asked how they could do that, and he said, "We just tell them to get someone else. We're not running a taxi service."

We started through an alley and Bob pointed out a whore-house on the second floor. There were lots of cars below, and he said that was why all the cars were parked in the alley. As we came to the end of the alley, one was illegally parked there. Bob got out and wrote a ticket for it. As he came back to the car and checked the hot-car sheet, he said, "Bet that one's wanted" and said sure it was. So they began to write the tickets. Chet said, "Maybe we should check if it's been reported." Bob said, "No it hasn't been; if it had been, there'd be tickets on it and there aren't any." They

*proceeded to write it up and then Chet asked me for the
license number. I gave it and he checked the sheet again and
said it was one digit off. They decided to call in and got a
response "Nothing on it. You got a run for larceny from a
building at————", and we were off to it. It was only an illegal parking ticket, then.*

*The larceny was less than two blocks away. The building
was an old one and we rang the building manager. A Negro
woman appeared holding a small child in her arms. She
said she was the manager and that there was $217 missing
from her apartment that she had collected in rents that day.
She led us into a small unkempt apartment on the first floor.
In an alcove was a desk table and she opened a drawer saying that she had kept the money in an insurance policy in
the desk drawer (under some papers) since that seemed like
the best hiding place. Chet asked for the information and
began by trying to get the denominations of the money
straight. He got a number of twenties, tens, fives and ones
and after some discussion got it to amount to $217. He
asked her if she had any idea who did it, and she said it
could have only been one of the boys who was there that
afternoon. She had a boy clean for her and he brought a
friend. They must have taken it after four o'clock. He got
the name, address, and phone number of the boy who
cleaned for her and she said she knew him since he was a
little boy. She didn't know much about the friend. There
were a few other routine questions. As we got ready to leave,
Bob said to her, "Well you know what you got to do now."
She said, "What?" He said, "You got to find a new hiding
place for the money when you collect it or take it to the
depository." She said she thought she had the best place and
he told her it was one of the worst. Anyone would look there
since it was right near her key board for the apartments and
where she made out her rent receipts. Chet asked her if she
was bonded and she said the place was bonded. As we
walked out, Bob told her that the Juvenile Bureau probably*

would be calling her about it. As we left the building, Bob told me that Goodman had recently bought the place and that it was better than it was. It used to be a collection of everything but that he had cleaned it out. "Notice how many apartments are vacant? When they took anything, they filled it up." He said Goodman seemed to be buying a lot of property around there as if he wanted a monopoly on it. We sat in the car a few minutes for Chet to make out a report. As we sat there, a panel truck pulled in front of the scout car and a boy jumped out. He rushed over to the window to say that someone had just tried to rob him and his mother in the alley and that they had come running down the alley that way. He said it had just happened three or four minutes ago so Bob asked him if he could identify them if he saw them and he said yes, so he told him to hop in the car and we would try to find them. We started to drive around. As we rounded a corner on Twelfth Street, two men were standing near a building. I couldn't quite see what they were doing but Bob stopped the car and called the older man over. He limped somewhat. Bob asked what he was doing and he said nothing. Bob said, "That's a lie," and told Chet to write a ticket on him for urinating against a building in public. Chet got out and we continued to drive. The boy stated that they didn't get his mother's purse, that the smaller boy had pushed him over and the bigger one had pulled at his mother's bag in which her purse was but didn't get it and ran off. He described them as two young guys. We drove around a bit more shining the light. Bob gave me a pad of paper and a flashlight and told me to get the usual information from the boy. I did so. We went back to let him off and pick Chet up. As Chet got in the car, Bob asked the man's name and then said, "I thought it was the same guy I wrote one on a few weeks ago." Chet said, "I didn't know you could write a ticket for that; I thought you had to take them in." The Negro man, by the way, had first tried to talk back and Bob had told him to quit arguing or he would take him in.

We then began to ride about again and Bob asked if I had ridden the cruiser. I said, not in number 10. He said, well they aren't much. "I think a man should have at least fifteen years of service to be on the cruiser. We got one here where together they don't have fifteen years. The people around here call it the "kiddie kar" and that's about it. It's a joke. On a cruiser you need men the people around here are afraid of. That's what they respect. We used to have a car here where all four were a bunch of sadists but they took them off. But the people around here ran from the cruiser. If they picked a guy up, they left a sadistic trademark. They generally broke the guy's nose; they had no trouble telling when they'd picked a guy up before."

Bob pointed out a blind pig on Twelfth as we went by. He went on, "All the guys on the cruiser around here want is to put in for citations. They'll put in for a citation for anything and they usually get it. If they have to take a man armed, they put in for a citation. If they have to run someone down in a chase, they put in for a citation. If they get shot at, they put in for a citation. But that's not the way a lot of guys figure it now. I had a young partner work with me a couple of months ago and we recovered a stolen auto from some boys who were armed. He thought we ought to put in for a citation and he asked the sergeant and the sergeant said we could and would probably get it. I refused to do it and he was plenty mad. I figured that's what we were getting paid for. For me a citation is something you get for doing something that is really out of the ordinary—out of the line of duty. If you're off duty and riding downtown with your family and you got some armed guys, well maybe you would put in them. But not for regular police work."

I asked him about what it was like under Edwards. He said, "Well, that's the sort of thing you better keep to yourself." I said that was probably so; I didn't know much about it. This opened him up and he said, "Well, there's no reason why you shouldn't say what you think. I'll tell you the truth. Under Commissioner Edwards, morale was as low in this

*department as it has ever been. It's a lot better now, let me
tell you. Edwards kept talking about crime going down
under him and the newspapers played that up but we knew
better out here—it was going up but the men weren't working. We just quit doing much work. We saw it all but no one
wanted to work for him. The attitude of Edwards and some
of the guys under him was, "We'll back you if you're right."
I don't need anyone to back me when I'm right. I can take
care of myself then. You need backing when you're wrong
and sometimes you're wrong, if you work hard. Around
here, you can end up wrong because you get into it. Take
like you are talking to someone and he argues with you and
you get a little mad and tell him to shut up, and he doesn't
and you get madder and tell him you'll knock him down if
he doesn't shut up. You've just got into it by that time.
You've just got two choices—you hit him or you back down.
And you're through around here if you back off, so you may
hit him. Well that's wrong, but you don't always stay out of
doing it the wrong way. That's when you need backing, if
there's a kick on it."*

*I asked him whether it was a lot better now. "We've got
the best bosses in the world. They let you pretty much alone
because they know you're busy. Once in a while they may
get on you like why aren't you writing more tickets, but they
got to say something if they're supervisors. You got to do
something to show that you're a supervisor. But mostly the
bosses let you alone. On midnights, they don't write you up
if you lay off the job for awhile and get a little rest. The attitude around here is you give us a good first four and you can
have the last four. There is none of that crap you find other
places."*

*We had a late lunch since we had to take it with a run.
Over lunch we talked about court time. Bob said that "court
times means good time out here. We go after all the court
time we can get since the bosses are good about giving us
full-time for it, even if it hurts. They let us back it up with*

days off. I even had a month's vacation last summer with my court time. The tenth is real good that way." I asked him if anyone lost court time since I knew they did other places and that in some districts in Detroit they had a hard time getting it. "We always get our court time and we arrange it so that we get it when we want it. I know this is the best district in the city that way. They take care of you."

A little later as we rode around, there was a call-your-station call. Chet answered since he was on that routine; it was for Bob. As he came back to the car, he said, "That was the lieutenant begging me to take three hours tomorrow and he'd let me have off on Monday. I said, I'd do four—I wanted that anyway."

We had a call to meet a man at an address. As we turned down the street, a car came speeding along and Bob pulled him over. He went to write him up and told Chet to take me and go find out what the man wanted. We went to a second-story apartment where a Negro man admitted us to a nice apartment. He told us that he didn't know whether we could help him or not. Chet asked him what the trouble was and he began to tell about how his wife always gets these calls from a man trying to date her and that there had been three of them tonight. She had let him listen on one of them. The guy talks in a muffled tone so you can't tell if he is someone you know. This has been going on for some time. Chet tried to get him to think about whom it might be but the man said they had no idea. Finally the man said, "Well, what can be done?" Chet said, "Well, I can't think of much. You could change your phone number and not list it in the phone book." The man demurred somewhat, saying that they had had that number for about fifteen years and they would hate to do that. Chet finally turned to me in desperation and said, "Is there anything else I could tell him?" I reassured him that having the number changed was probably the simplest way of taking care of the matter and that, since there were no threats, probably nothing else should be done. I didn't think it important to bring up the whole question of whether she should try to date the man, have DB lay a trap for him, and so on. Just then the phone rang and the man motioned to us thinking it was the caller, but it turned out to be for his son. When he completed that conversation, he began all over on the anonymous caller. I finally started toward the door with Chet coming up gradually behind me and we made it down the stairs with the man saying they'd probably have the phone number changed. Bob would have cooled the man sooner I'm sure. DB never investigates unless a major threat is involved. When Chet talked about it with Bob, his comment was, "It probably was her boyfriend."

We began to move about the district again when the radio said to check on a missing girl. Bob commented, "That's the way it goes; every time you begin to do some police work, you get stuck with this stuff." He went on to say: "I guess 90 percent of all police work is bullshit. All most people want is a shoulder to lean on."

When we got to the place, it was a second-story apartment. A boy of about twenty-one met us at the door and said it was his twelve-year-old sister. There were three other girls from eighteen to twenty-five or so in the place—his sisters, he said—a boy of about ten and two boys under two years (seemingly the children of his sisters). He recounted: "My sister just got home from the Training School today and the worker downtown told my mother if she left to call her right away. She left about an hour ago and we called my mother and she said to call you." Chet asked where her mother was and he said working and gave Chet the telephone number. Chet was a little confused about what to do and turned to Bob. Bob asked how long the girl had been gone and he said an hour. He asked whether they thought she'd be back and they said no. He told Chet to talk with the mother and Chet called her. He had the obvious talk with her about her being gone, etc. Finally, he turned to Bob and said, "You talk with her." Bob began and talked with *her and discovered the girl had run away once before that day and had come back about two hours later. He listened more. Finally, he said, "Well, look, it isn't curfew yet and she can be out until curfew time. Why don't you wait until an hour after curfew, or until you come home (that's about eleven o'clock then) and then if she still isn't home, call the number at the Women's Division downtown and talk with them about it, and then, if you still want us to list her as a missing person, why give us a call again and we'll come out and list her as a missing person." There was some little discussion of this and agreement that she would do that. Meanwhile Chet had begun to make out a missing person report. Bob told him to forget about it as they wouldn't list her as missing unless they called back. The boy said that his sister probably wouldn't come back as she said when she left that she was going, that this wasn't her home anymore, that she was on her own. As we left, Bob said that they grew up fast around here, that she probably was out on the streets now, looking for a trick for the night. I made a mental note of the fact that the gestalt of the situation suggested this to some extent (no father in the home, sisters with young children living in the extended kin household, and now a young sister running to the streets at twelve, perhaps only to return when she was pregnant, and yet this household was by no means at the bottom and a brother was taking some responsibility in it).*

As we rode around, we talked some about the area. Bob said, "In this kind of area you can't get too far away from the people, because you depend upon them in lots of ways. Take the prostitutes in this area. You aren't going to get rid of them. You know most of them and when you see them, you talk with them. You tell them they got to expect to work Thursday, Friday and Saturday without being taken in—that we'll let them alone then without bothering them but that they got to expect to take a fall once every couple of weeks on Sunday, Monday, Tuesday, or Wednesday. They almost all go along with that. Sometimes you'll come up to one and tell her she's got to go in and she'll say, 'OK but let me turn a couple of tricks first so I got enough for court,' and she'll tell you that she'll meet you at a restaurant, say at ten o'clock. And you let her go and she'll turn up and get in the car with you and go in. They cooperate.

"Some officers don't understand an area like this and they don't get on as well. They don't get information when they need it. If you want to be able to find things out when you need to, you got to stay on the right side of these people. A lot of officers when they knock off a still will take an axe to the barrels. My partners and I don't usually do that. We round up as many bottles around the place as we can, wash them out, and fill them up and put them in the trunk first. Then later we take them around to the people who help us out and they really appreciate it. They'll give you tips and tell you things when you need to know."

We got the last run of the night—a man in a hall in an apartment building. We went to it. It was a nice appearing enough building with new brocade on the walls in the lobby. An old woman on the first floor answered the door and said that someone kept knocking at her door and she was afraid to open it. Bob told her OK, we'd check the building. He told Chet to go up one side, he'd take the other and for me to watch the elevator and the lobby. Chet came down in a moment and said he'd seen the guy come out of an apartment on the third floor so there was no reason to check him further. Bob came down a few minutes later having found no one and saying, "That lock on the back door is an expensive one not to hold anything. He may have gone out that way or it's just a bunch of kids living in here and annoying her for some reason."

We rode slowly toward the station. As we did, Bob began to talk about how the "colored" treated their kids in the area, even those who were fairly well off. He said, "They're not like us. They spend a lot on themselves for cars, clothes, liquor and living it up. They spend almost nothing on their kids. I used to work every Christmas eve and go home sick and it just wasn't Christmas for me. On Christmas eve you'd get these calls to these houses about noisy parties and you'd go in. Everyone would be drunk and disorderly and all the expensive liquor bottles all over the place and there would be an old tree with almost nothing on it and probably not two dollars worth of presents under it for the kids. They'd spend all that money for the grownups and have a big party Christmas eve and then treat the kids like that. I got so disgusted with it, Christmas didn't mean a thing and my family felt it. Last year I told the lieutenant, I just wouldn't work Christmas eve and I took the family to midnight mass and we had a real Christmas for a change. I'm not going to work it again. The kids just don't get a break around here."

As we headed toward the station we went through an alley. A car was parked illegally in the alley so that we had to turn around to get out. Bob said, "Too bad that's an out-of-state or we'd write it." I asked why they didn't bother with out-of-state and he gave the usual reply that it was too much work to do anything with it after you wrote it up.

As we came to the station, it was about quarter of twelve. We parked outside the brick wall where several other cars were waiting, Bob observing that it was a little early to be going in. We waited about ten minutes while they did up the reports. I looked at the run sheet for the month. They average about one arrest a night with about three felonies a week, as arrests.

We see, then, that it is incumbent upon a police officer to enter upon a variety of social stages, encounter the actors, determine their roles, and figure out the plot. Often, before they can act, the police must uncover the "plot" and identify the roles and behavior of the actors. This is true even in emergency situations where an officer is expected to assess the situation almost immediately and make judgments as to what he must do. The fate of the actors and the situation in such cases may reside with the police.

The feature of police work most commonly emphasized is

the necessity *to assert authority*. This is closely related to two other facets of the work situation: the willingness of the client to cooperate with the police, and the necessity to utilize force to control the client. Police must be prepared to assert authority when the client is unwilling to cooperate, and, if necessary, use coercive authority, including physical force.

Clients of professionals are not always cooperative. The teacher is faced with unwilling pupils, the psychiatrist with a resident patient, and the judge with a hostile witness or defendant. Yet the situation is different for the police. When any practicing professional is faced with a particularly violent client, he can call the police. The police must cope with any and all clients regardless of their willingness to be processed.

In police work, frequently an officer is confronted with a dual set of clients—those who call the police and those who are to be "policed." Those who call are prepared to accept his authority; those who are to be policed often do not. In the latter situation, the officer may have to assert authority. It is not surprising, therefore, that on entering a situation, an officer typically takes command by asserting authority.

Unlike most professionals, who deal with clients who are preprocessed to accept the authority of the professional when he enters the situation, the police officer must *establish* his authority. The uniform, badge, truncheon, and arms all may play a role in asserting authority. Yet, it appears that the police exercise command in most situations simply by behaving as men in authority.

Police patrol work calls for *intervention* in social situations, where the problem for an officer is to gain control of the situation. This generally means he must establish his legitimate right to intervene.

The way in which the officer establishes his authority, as already noted, varies depending on the social setting, the participants in it, and the officer himself. Two types of social situations, in particular, make the establishment of authority difficult. Whenever there is disorder or conflict in a situation when the police officer intervenes, the officer must find a way to gain control by establishing *order*. When one or more parties to the conflict rejects the officer's right to intervene, he regards this as a challenge to *his* authority. When an officer is confronted by calls about family troubles, neighborhood disputes, and business disturbances, as well as more general situations of public disorder, the success of his intervention will depend largely on his authority and skill in establishing order in the situation. Generally, this must be accomplished without resort to force, although the threat of force may be ever-present.

It is reasonable, then, that the most common complaint officers in our studies voice about citizens is their failure to show respect for authority. Perhaps the main reason police officers generally seek deference toward their authority is that it assures order and control in the situations they are expected to handle. Moreover, it is their major means of control apart from the use of force or threat of coercion (e.g., threats to arrest).

The second important aspect of intervention is the degree of *social* support for the officer in the situation. When the officer intervenes on his *own* authority, as is typically the case in on-view police work, he is likely not to have such support. More typically, when he is dispatched to an encounter, he can usually assume the social support of the citizens who mobilized him. Yet, even then, it sometimes happens that these citizens are not always present in the situation when the officer intervenes. This often happens with reports of juveniles causing trouble in public places, calls reporting neighborhood disturbances, victimless crimes, and requests for intervention on behalf of organizations seeking the removal of large numbers of persons.

Our observation of police and citizen encounters in high-crime-rate areas of Boston, Chicago, and Washington provide some indication of the difficulties an officer faces in establishing authority in encounters with citizens. It is difficult to determine whether an officer's or a citizen's behavior initiated the tone or action in an encounter. When, for example, we observed that an officer was "hostile" at the same time that a citizen was "antagonistic" toward the officer, it was unclear whether the officer was reacting to the citizen or, vice versa.

Observers described the general emotional state of the citizen in encounters as agitated, calm, or very detached. We assumed that in situations where a citizen was agitated, the officer would have greater difficulty in establishing his authority. Observers also characterized the general demeanor of the citizen toward authority in the situation in terms of very deferential, civil, or antagonistic toward authority. The officer's behavior toward a citizen was characterized as good-humored or jovial, businesslike or routine, brusque or authoritarian, or hostile or provocative. Tables 1.5 and 1.6 present the officer's behavior in relation to the citizen's conduct (rather than the other way around), since the normative and role expectation is that police officers will respond in an equally "professional" manner to *all* citizens, regardless of their behavior. If an officer behaves with hostility, for example, from a normative standpoint, the citizen's behavior toward him is irrelevant. Even where the specific form of the citizen's behavior must determine the officer's behavior (viz., where force is necessary to arrest or self-defense), the officer is expected to use only the amount of force incident to a proper arrest. Of special interest then are the conditions under which officers conform to or deviate from such normative expectations.

The relationship between officers and citizens is a summation of the behavior of each officer and each citizen toward, or in the presence of, one another in an encounter. The behavior of a maximum of five citizens in transactions with

Table 1.5

Percentage Distribution by General Emotional State and Race of Citizens, by Conduct of Police Officer toward Citizen and Type of Mobilization of the Police

General emotional state of citizen	Race	Total number of mobilizations*		Percentage by general emotional state		Conduct of police officer toward citizen												Total percentage	
						Good-humored or jovial		Business-like or routinized		Ridiculed or belittled		Authoritarian or hostile and other(s)		Brusque or authoritarian		Hostile or provocative			
		D	OV	D	OV	D	OV	D	OV	D	OV	D	OV	D	OV	D	OV	D	OV
Agitated	White	1203	222	28	31	16	5	67	52	7	9	5	12	4	20	1	2	100	100
	Negro	2379	209	31	19	10	11	76	54	6	10	2	12	4	12	1	2	100	100
Calm	White	2867	448	66	63	25	20	65	63	3	5	1	3	4	4	1	5	100	100
	Negro	4708	729	61	67	13	12	81	69	3	6	2	7	3	8	—	1	100	100
Very detached	White	221	23	5	3	13	9	69	43	5	4	3	4	10	39	1	—	100	100
	Negro	590	121	8	11	11	8	81	72	2	5	2	7	4	3	—	5	100	100
Not ascertained	White	59	15	1	2	3	—	78	67	—	—	—	7	5	7	14	20	100	100
	Negro	80	36	1	3	6	—	90	78	—	14	—	—	4	8	—	—	100	100

*D = Dispatches; OV = On views

Table 1.6

Percentage Distribution by General Demeanor and Race of Citizen, by Conduct of Police Officer toward Citizen and Type of Mobilization of the Police

General demeanor of citizen	Race	Total number of mobilizations*		Percentage by demeanor of citizen		Good-humored or jovial		Business-like or routinized		Ridiculed or belittled		Authoritarian or hostile and other(s)		Brusque or authoritarian		Hostile or provocative		Total percentage	
		D	OV	D	OV	D	OV	D	OV	D	OV	D	OV	D	OV	D	OV	D	OV
Total	White	5012	709	100	100														
	Negro	7766	1153	100	100														
Very deferential	White	547	81	11	11	35	19	56	52	3	6	3	13	2	10	1	—	100	100
	Negro	880	139	11	12	23	13	71	61	3	14	1	4	2	6	—	2	100	100
Civil	White	3945	488	79	69	21	17	68	65	4	5	2	4	4	7	1	2	100	100
	Negro	5944	766	77	67	11	9	82	74	3	4	1	5	3	7	—	1	100	100
Antagonistic	White	318	112	6	16	8	2	43	34	21	10	10	10	16	31	2	13	100	100
	Negro	544	175	7	15	7	4	60	52	14	19	3	8	14	14	2	3	100	100
Not ascertained	White	202	28	4	4	9	11	79	67	3	4	—	—	7	4	2	14	100	100
	Negro	398	73	5	6	7	4	88	88	1	—	1	4	3	4	—	—	100	100

*D = Dispatches; OV = On views

a maximum of two police officers, and vice versa, is described for each type of mobilization. A maximum of ten relationships could be described for any police encounter with citizens. The total number of relationships, of course, generally is smaller for the typical police-citizen encounter.

Although a majority of citizens can be characterized as calm or very detached and as civil or very deferential in encounters with the police, a substantial minority of roughly 3 in 10 were agitated in encounters, and 1 in 10 could be considered antagonistic toward the police. As table 1.7 shows, most of the antagonism toward the police in encounters comes from persons who are offenders or who stand in a close relationship to the offender in the situation. Almost 15 percent of all offenders as compared with roughly 3 percent of all other persons in police and citizen encounters were antagonistic toward the police. As expected, antagonism toward the police was higher in on-view than in dispatched encounters, largely owing to the fact that the police are most likely to intervene on their own authority where there is an offender, and offenders are likely to respond antagonistically toward police intervention.

It is also clear that police officers depart from a model of professional or bureaucratic handling of citizens. Although in almost three-fourths of all encounters, the police behaved in a businesslike or routine civil fashion toward citizens, and in an additional 15 percent they were more personal in demeanor, expressing humor or joviality, in 11 percent of all encounters they were hostile, authoritarian, or derisive of citizens.

In general, policemen are more hostile or authoritarian and more likely to ridicule citizens of both races when, as seen in table 1.5, the citizens are agitated than when they are calm or detached. This becomes even clearer if we take officer rather than citizen behavior as the statistical base. The citizen was described as agitated or excited in 48 per-

Table 1.7

Percentage Distribution by General Demeanor and Race of Citizens According to the Role of the Citizen in Encounter with the Police and Type of Mobilization of the Police

General demeanor of citizen	Race	Role of citizen in police encounter											
		Complainant, or in complainant group*		Offender, or in offender group		Victim, or in victim group		Informant		Bystander		Not ascertained	
		D	OV	D	OV	D	OV	D	OV	D	OV	D	OV
Very deferential	White	12	23	7	9	14	15	9	—	3	8	4	†
	Negro	13	15	11	15	20	4	12	†	6	—	15	†
Civil	White	83	73	73	66	74	80	87	100	73	72	87	†
	Negro	80	83	68	65	69	88	81	†	68	65	77	†
Antagonistic	White	3	—	13	20	1	—	2	—	4	—	2	†
	Negro	3	2	16	14	3	—	3	†	5	5	2	†
Not ascertained	White	2	4	7	5	11	5	2	—	20	20	7	†
	Negro	4	—	5	6	8	8	4	†	21	30	6	†
Total number of mobilizations	White	1697	26	988	311	304	20	254	11	386	35	55	1
	Negro	1950	52	1342	508	441	25	243	9	691	95	54	1
Percentage of mobilizations	White	46	6	27	77	8	5	7	3	10	9	4	‡
	Negro	41	8	28	74	9	4	5	1	15	14	1	‡
Total Percentage	White	100	100	100	100	100	100	100	100	100	100	100	†
	Negro	100	100	100	100	100	100	100	†	100	100	100	†

*D = Dispatches; OV = On views
†Percentage not calculated where there are fewer than 10 observations.
‡Less than 0.5 percent

cent of all encounters where an officer was hostile, 35 percent where he was brusque or authoritarian, 42 percent in which he openly ridiculed a citizen, and 57 percent where the officer subtly ridiculed or belittled a citizen.

Officers are far more likely to be hostile, brusque, and derisive when citizens are antagonistic, rather than respectful toward them. Table 1.6 shows that this is even more characteristic of citizen and officer transactions in on-view than in dispatched encounters. When white citizens, for example, were antagonistic in on-view situations, the police were hostile, brusque, or derisive in 64 percent of the encounters. The proportion is somewhat lower for Negroes, 44 percent.

Again, considering officer behavior as a statistical base, it is clear that officer behavior is closely related to citizen behavior. Although the police openly ridiculed citizens in only 2 percent of all cases where citizens were antagonistic, these cases represented 43 percent of the times that officers behaved in this manner. Similarly, while the police were hostile toward only 3 percent of the antagonistic citizens, 35 percent of the behavior was directed toward antagonistic citizens.

Two conclusions about the assertion of police authority may be drawn from tables 1.5 and 1.6. Although most of all kinds of police behavior is directed toward citizens who behave civilly toward them, a disproportionate amount of "unprofessional" or "negative" police conduct is directed toward citizens who refuse to defer to their authority. Secondly, citizens who behave antagonistically toward the police are more likely to be treated in a hostile, authoritarian or belittling manner by the police than citizens who behave with civility or who extend deference.

The most direct measure of interference with police authority occurs when the police exercise the right of arrest. At law, there is provision for charging a citizen with resisting an arrest in addition to the charge for which he is under arrest. Furthermore, any citizen interfering with an arrest is open to a charge of interference with an arrest. Booking on a charge of resisting an arrest or interfering with an arrest, as for all arrests, is a matter of officer discretion. Official data therefore are open to the criticism that they represent a police labeling process.

In our observational study of police and citizen encounters in high-crime-rate areas, observers characterized the behavior of offenders toward arresting officers as violent or aggressive, disgruntled or sullen, passive and unexpressive, or cooperative. If we consider all offenders who behaved in a violent or aggressive way toward officers during or following the arrest as open to charges of resisting an arrest, we find that 12 percent of all persons under the arrest were open to such charges.

Observers also characterized the verbal behavior of the offender during the arrest situation. It was classified as insulting or explosive, argumentative, passive or quiet, and good-natured or jovial. Almost one-half of all offenders under arrest, who were transported to the station for booking, were insulting or explosive (16 percent) or argued with officers (31 percent). In other words, 1 in every 2 citizens under arrest will challenge an officer's authority, at least verbally. Indeed, only 1 in 5 citizens under arrest was characterized by observers as cooperative with the police.

Given this amount of resistance, we asked observers to characterize the degree of force used against the offender. Nine percent of the offenders were handled with gross force involving some physical coercion or threat (physical assault, handcuffs, etc.), though not necessarily an undue use of such force. An additional 42 percent were treated with firm handling, generally moving the offender about by holding him by the arm, prodding him with a nightstick, or surrounding him with several police officers. Only 1 of every 2 offenders was free to move about in the presence of officers. Generally, police officers regard citizen resistance as routine, and our percentages agree. Because of this, officers don't usually file a resisting charge against an offender. Inasmuch as we did not follow many of our offenders through the booking process, we were unable to determine the conditions under which a charge of resisting actually was filed. We know that, in each of the cities, charges of resisting an arrest were relatively uncommon in situations that might have warranted such charges. Contrary to what many police officers believe, an officer generally does not cover himself for resorting to physical coercion (even to the point where the offender sustains some injury) by charging an offender with resisting an arrest.

An understanding of the conditions under which law-enforcement officers and organizations define and process citizens as *interfering with* or *resisting an arrest* may be gained from our study of such charges in the San Francisco Police Department for the years 1959 to 1964. For the years 1959 to 1963, the police department data include only those charges where interfering or resisting was either the primary or additional charge lodged against the offender. For the first nine months of 1964, the data include *all* charges, regardless of the number, lodged against the offender. While there is some variation in the percentage of arrests involving such charges throughout the period, there was no evidence of an ultimate increase in arrests with a charge of interfering or resisting.

The large majority of cases where a person was charged with resisting an arrest involved some other charges as well. It is often presumed that in the more serious crime situations, particularly where the offender is armed, citizens are more likely to resist arrest. The data on the offense charged when there also was a charge of interfering or resisting hardly support such a contention:

Offense	Percentage
Crimes against public justice	5.3
Part I crimes against the person	15.5
Part I crimes against property	3.3
Crimes against the person, decency, and public morals	2.0
Crimes against the public peace	12.9
Drunkenness	35.8
Vagrancy	2.0
Malicious mischief	1.1
Municipal-code violations	1.5
Vehicle-code violations	6.9
Traffic-code violations	2.3
Minors in violation of laws	4.0
Warrants	3.1
Narcotics	1.8
All other	2.5
Total	100.0

Thirty-six percent of the charges of resisting or interfering with an arrest occurred in situations where the charge was drunkenness. The police usually pick these people up in the streets, on skid rows, in the areas of homeless men, and similar life situations. These types of offenders have little to lose by resisting arrest, and, under the influence of alcohol, they often become more aggressive in their behavior. They are generally arrested for creating a disturbance, lying in a public place, or otherwise engaging in what is described as "nuisance" behavior. Crimes involving peace disturbances accounted for an additional 13 percent. Thus, one-half of all arrests for resisting or interfering were coupled with charges for misdemeanors where the public peace or order was "threatened."

Part I crimes against persons and property involved only 19 percent of all charges. The bulk of these were for assault or battery.

Traffic, and vehicle-code violations—generally matters of on-view police preventive work—accounted for more than 9 percent of all charges, and the serving of warrants an additional 3 percent.

Apart from situations of mass disorder, where charges of interfering with or resisting an arrest are common, these charges usually are lodged in situations police define as related to their peace-keeping functions: the preservation of order or the restoration of order. Most frequently, the situations involve minor offenses that, at law and in the view of officers, are regarded as "offending public sensibilities." They often involve a "disorderly person," a label open to rather broad discretion as to charges. The other main type of situation leading to such charges is one where conflict exists between parties and the officer intervenes to restore order.

Both the citizen's behavior of resisting or interfering with an arrest and the officer's behavior in preferring such charges can be understood by examining the legitimacy of authority in such situations. There are several reasons why this is so. First, arrests for minor violations are more likely to provoke citizens to claim that authority is being exercised *arbitrarily* and *unjustly,* because many others escape arrest in such situations. Facts may be more controversial in such situations, particularly as revealed by complainants or when there is disagreement between a complainant and an alleged offender. Furthermore, bystanders are more likely to interfere for precisely the same reasons, a judgment or feeling that the officer is making an "arbitrary arrest," an arrest on grounds about the persons, rather than the facts related to the offense; grounds of race or class position, or other matters relating to the status of the offenders. Indeed, often these bystanders are not "offended" by such conduct; they are culpable.

Secondly, in situations involving the enforcement of public safety, peace, and order, the police officer often inter-

venes on his *own* authority (he discovers or comes upon it
on view), rather than on the authority of a complainant who
has called the communications center. Indeed, when officers
intervene in such situations on their own authority, they
cannot begin with the usual queries to parties about "What's
the trouble here?" or "Who called the police?" Rather they
assert authority by such means as commands: "break-it-up,"
"move on," or even more commonly "get your ass out of
here." When officers do intervene based on a complaint to
the department, the complainant often is not present on
the scene when the police arrive. This is particularly likely
when the complainant fears that the disturbance might
involve violence. In such cases, there is no one present to
support the legitimacy of police intervention. Entering on
his own authority or without the support of others, who may
have mobilized him, an officer is more vulnerable to both
resistance in dealing with the offender and interference from
bystanders or other participants in the situation.

A third problem is, when a police officer enters a situation
on his own authority (on view) it is often because he sees a
disturbance of some kind in progress or a flagrant violation
of the law that he regards as meriting intervention, even if
it is only a misdemeanor or violation of a minor provision of
the code. Indeed, such situations are often ones where aggression is taking place, either verbal or physical, and in
these cases, there is a higher probability that an officer will
encounter resistance to arrest or interference. In other situations, as where warrants are served, the officer comes without warning upon the offender to perform a task that is likely
to make the person hostile. Actually, as we shall note later,
officers are not unaware of the dangers of violence toward
them in on-view situations, and they seek ways to avoid intervention in them. It is partly for this reason that they dislike one-man cars, since they are disinclined to risk asking
for assistance every time they come upon an on-view situation.

There is one other matter that may affect the development of interfering or resisting the work of a police officer in such settings. When a police officer enters solely on his own authority (without a complaint), the department is unaware that he is intervening unless he radios the department that he is doing so. Officers often do not. Indeed, if they are on foot patrol or plainclothes, generally they are not equipped with radios. Since the department learns of the situation only when and if the officer chooses to inform it, he is free of the constraint and authority of a command dispatch. Lacking the supervision of authority, officers may be more likely to act in ways that provoke interference or resistance from persons in the situation.

There is strong support in the San Francisco data that situations where the officer intervenes on his own authority (on views) more commonly involve charges of interfering with or resisting an arresting officer. Of all charges for interfering or resisting, 47 percent occurred in on-view situations. Our observational studies show that only 14 percent of all police-citizen encounters were on-view encounters. If one assumes the rate is much the same for San Francisco, then clearly situations where the officer intervenes on his own authority more likely elicit such charges, if not behavior leading to such charges.

It must also be noted that on-view situations in and of themselves were more likely, in our observational studies, to lead to an arrest, largely owing to the high proportion of traffic offenses among all on views. For reasons noted above, traffic offenses are generative of charges of resisting an arrest. In our studies, 31 percent of all arrests were on-view arrests. Even accounting for the fact that arrests are higher where the officer intervenes on his own authority, such intervention is more likely to bring charges of interfering with or resisting arrest.

It is difficult to determine, of course, whether this resistance in on-view settings is due primarily to the nature of the situation or to the fact that the officers enter without prior legitimacy in the situation (there is generally no complainant who has mobilized them, though a complainant may emerge in the situation as a victim). There is some evidence for the argument that lack of prior legitimacy is a factor, if we assume that interference with a police officer is more likely to occur when legitimacy is questioned, while resistance is more likely to arise simply from hostility (apart from questioning legitimacy of authority as such). In table 1.5, we note that when the interfering charges are considered separately, a somewhat higher proportion (54 percent) than that for all interfering and resisting arrests (47 percent) occurred in on-view situations. Correlatively, of the resisting charges, proportionally fewer occurred in on-view settings (43 percent). Looked at another way, in 33 percent of the on-view settings, the charge was interfering with rather than resisting arrest; this was true for only 24 percent in all dispatched cases (28 percent of all arrests were for charges of interfering). Nonetheless, these differences are not large.

When legitimacy of authority is at stake and there is resistance to authority, physical force may be involved in making an arrest. The use of physical force inevitably introduces the risk of injury to both the arrested person and the officer. Indeed, the threat of injury undoubtedly serves as a constraint on the use of force by officers, although we have no way of assessing such a constraint. Our data for San Francisco show that in 11 percent of all arrests for interfering or resisting, an officer was injured to the degree that he required medical attention and usually some sick leave as well.

Two rather striking facts that relate to our argument about the legitimacy of authority emerge from an analysis of the injury rate of officers in making arrests where they also charge interference or resistance to arrest.

The first is that the large majority of injuries to officers occurs with charges of interfering with an officer rather than resisting arrest. Almost three-fourths (73 percent) of all injuries to officers occurred when the charge was interference with an officer. Since only 28 percent of all charges of interfering with an officer involved injury to an officer, it appears that assault, itself, against officers, whether or not it resulted in injury, provoked charges of interference. It is possible, of course, that officers are more likely to charge interfering rather than resisting arrest when they sustain an injury. However, the persons charged with interference are not usually the parties involved in the situation which prompted the intervention, but ra⁴her citizens who were present. When such persons question the legitimacy of police intervention and a police officer reacts to control their behavior, more serious conflict may ensue as each party attempts to gain control of the situation. This results more often in injury to the officer. Another possibility is that in such situations, a group often confronts the officer and the sheer power of physical conflict is more likely to eventuate in injury to the officer.

The second striking fact is that injury is greater in on-view than dispatch mobilizations. While 60 percent of the injuries occurred in on-view situations, only 46 percent of all arrests for interfering or resisting were in on-view situations. Yet as the tabulation below clearly shows, it is the on-view interference with an officer that is most likely to result in injury:

Mobilization and charge	Percentage of all injured	Percentage of all charges
On view		
Interfering with an officer	48	15
Resisting an officer	12	31
Total on view	60	46
Dispatch		
Interfering with an officer	25	13
Resisting arrest	15	41
Total dispatch	40	54

Almost one-half of all injuries to police officers occurred in the on-view setting where the charge was interfering with an officer.

The question arises whether we can predict more precisely the situations where this will arise. Considering all on-view interfering charges, we note that these injuries tend to occur at this rate for Part I crimes against the person; crimes against the public peace; minors in violation of laws; and, to a lesser degree, drunkenness and vagrancy. It should be noted that the risk of injury is much lower for these crimes in the resisting arrest offenses, whether on view or dispatched.

We conclude then that these crimes are the highest injury-risk-offense situations where the additional charge is interfering with an officer rather than resisting arrest. The condition of interference appears to be more important in determining the risk than is the condition of mobilization, whether on-view or dispatched, though the risk is somewhat greater for these offenses in the on-view setting. Hence, we must look for something in these situations when the additional charge is interfering that accounts for the higher injury rate, if we are to be sure it is something more than the charge most commonly placed when an officer is injured. That something seems to be the assertion of authority and its definition as "illegitimate."

II

POLICING EVERYDAY LIFE

Local police forces in America have a broad legal mandate to enforce the criminal law and preserve public peace. Implicit in this mandate is an obligation to police everyday life—matters that arise in the daily lives and activities of citizens within a community. However, the duties of the police involve far more than matters of everyday life. For example, the police operate as a paramilitary organization in controlling behavior in mass disorders. Many violations of the commonweal transcend local and state jurisdictions such as espionage, counterfeiting, or illegal entry into the country, and are not police matters in everyday life. In America these violations are commonly delegated to specialized law-enforcement agencies at the federal level.

Many citizens consider the function of the police in everyday life to extend beyond their law-enforcement and peace-keeping roles. The lower classes, in particular, call upon the police to perform a variety of services. They depend upon police assistance in times of trouble, crises, and indecision. To whom does one turn when a family member is missing? Who answers the questions of strangers, citizens, or businessmen in need of information? Who responds to accidents and emergencies? Often the police. Such roles of assistance are as much a police function as are coercive roles of authority. Service is inextricably bound up with public order and law enforcement. The police, in fact, receive more calls requesting assistance in noncriminal matters or reporting a crime that has already occurred than calls requiring immediate intervention to save victims of crimes.

Citizens usually bring matters to police attention by telephoning, signaling a scout car or officer on foot, or appearing in person at a police station. The police department deals with such requests as a *reactive organization*. The department may respond to telephone reports by radio dispatch of officers. However, most other mobilizations of the police by citizens, when not ignored, require face-to-face encounters with citizens.

The police also acquire information by intervening in the lives of citizens on their own initiative. In this capacity, they serve as a *proactive organization,* pursuing matters through investigative activities, preventive patrol, and direct intervention in the lives of citizens (including the techniques of stopping, frisking, searching, and questioning). Excluding motor vehicle violations, proactive policing generally brings a substantially smaller proportion of incidents to police attention than does citizen mobilization.

Whether or not the police are mobilized by citizens has enormous consequences for the *legitimacy* of police intervention. Citizens mobilize the police for what they regard as crises or important matters. What the citizen generally regards as a crisis is necessarily routine to the police; it becomes part of their *regular* work and follows routines. Likewise, police intervention in the lives of citizens by such means as detaining citizens for questions—regarded by police as routine preventive or investigative work necessary to their role as agents of crime control—are often regarded by citizens as harassment, infringement upon individual rights, or unauthorized intervention.

Citizens and police act within the law-enforcement system in a variety of roles. A consideration of these roles and their effect on law-enforcement organization sheds some light on the policing of everyday life.

Citizens may be found as adversaries of one another when some, the victims or complainants, charge others with violations and call the police. Or, citizens may call the police when they believe a crime has occurred, although a violator is not known. In these situations, the citizen is generally seen by the police, in the role of complainant, suspect, or offender. However, citizens may also fail to fulfill their civic duty to call the police about criminal matters. In this sense, citizens may be regarded as enforcers or nonenforcers of the law and its moral order. They may also behave as informants, providing useful information to the police, or as adversaries, making complaints about police.

Thus, the relationships between citizens and the police are complex. Citizens who find themselves in antagonistic relationships with each other may or may not call the police. They may have an antagonistic relationship with the police. Or, their relationships with one another and with the police can be ones where they mutually sustain the law and support one another. A civil society depends upon the latter.

The nature of police-citizen relations in everyday life has certain implications for a civil society. The obligations involved in the policing of everyday life are so numerous and varied precisely because the police are largely an organization reacting to the demands of citizens. As such, citizens can exercise considerable control over law enforcement by discretionary decisions as nonenforcers of the law.

Discretionary Decisions of Citizens to Mobilize the Police

While citizen reports control the input of crime information into police departments, often citizens choose not to report even their own victimization to the police. Of course, a citizen's decision is sometimes influenced by his status as victim as well as violator (as in consensual crimes). Nevertheless, it is curious that even in many of the most serious situations, the victims fail to mobilize the police.

There have been studies of the failure of citizens to report crimes to the police in an attempt to understand the patterns of crime in society and to assess the validity and reliability of police statistics. These unreported cases are commonly regarded as the "dark figure of crimes." Recent studies show that much crime in the United States goes unreported to the police. The National Opinion Research Center sample survey of United States households showed that, in 1965, more than half of all crimes and 38 percent of all UCR-Index crimes against residents went unreported to the police. Sample surveys in high-crime-rate areas of Boston, Chicago, and Washington, D.C. generally indicated even higher rates of underreporting of major crimes. For the eight high-crime-rate precincts in these cities combined, the survey estimates for Index offenses was four times that of the rates known to the police.[1] Other evidence from studies of the validity and reliability of surveys in estimating unreported crime indicates that these estimates are conservative.

Much crime in American society is committed against businesses and other organizations. Embezzlement, fraud, and forgery are the most common crimes committed against them, but the more serious crimes of robbery, burglary, and larceny are also often directed against them. Other less serious crimes that frequently occur within or against these places include vandalism, drunkenness, disorderly conduct, and assault. In these crimes against businesses and other organizations, the owner, manager, or some employee of the establishment is usually the complainant.

Our surveys for the National Crime Commission and the Small Business Administration on crimes against businesses and other organizations indicate that many crimes against establishments also go unreported. This is particularly true

1. Albert D. Biderman, "Surveys of Population Samples for Estimating Crime Incidence," *The Annals of the American Academy of Political and Social Science* 374 (November 1967): 16–33.

for shoplifting offenses, employee theft, and passing bad checks. Often, even burglary goes unreported.[2]

These facts more than suggest that official police statistics on crime may not be true indicators of crime rates. They tell us that the many victimized citizens who—either as private persons or as members of organizations—fail to exercise their civic responsibility to report crimes to the police, greatly limit the power of the police in everyday life. The desire to understand why citizens do not exercise their power to mobilize the police leads us to inquire into the conditions under which they do and do not call the police.

A major factor in the failure to report crimes against property is property insurance. When a person is not insured against losses, or his losses are not covered by a policy (often the case for the poor), he fails to report because he sees no personal gain in doing so. Even with insurance coverage, many businesses, and some citizens, fail to report because they fear their policy may be cancelled or not renewed, or there will be a future rate increase. These are the reasons most often given by businessmen who have already made claims or who operate businesses in high-crime-rate areas.[3] Conversely, insurance coverage also operates as an incentive for citizens to make inputs into the law-enforcement system, since some people assume that to collect on their insurance they must report losses to the police. Although data are lacking, there is reason to believe that some of the increase in crimes known to the police may be a simple con-

2. See Albert J. Reiss, Jr., "Measurement of the Nature and Amount of Crime," in President's Commission on Law Enforcement and the Administration of Justice, *Studies in Crime and Law Enforcement in Major Metropolitan Areas,* Field Surveys III, vol. 1, sec. 1 (Washington, D.C.: USGPO, 1967); and Reiss, "Appendix A, Field Survey," in *Crime against Small Business: A Report of the Small Business Administration,* U.S. Senate Document 91–14, 91st Cong., 1st sess., April 3, 1969.

3. Reiss, in *Crime against Small Business,* pp. 131–43.

sequence of the advent of the Homeowner's Policy, which extends insurance coverage for many crimes that formerly went unreported.

These data on insurance coverage strongly suggest that one's civic obligation to mobilize the police against crimes of property is often subverted by questions of personal gain. The importance of personal gain as a factor in mobilizing victims to report crimes was evident in the Washington, D.C. study of victimization by crime. The ratio was 1 in 3 for citizens who said they had not reported a crime against them or their property because they felt nothing could be done about it by the police, and they therefore stood to gain nothing.[4] Clearly evident in many replies was the assumption that most crimes remain unsolved by the police.

Another major cause of failure to report crimes is a negative attitude toward the police. Citizens may fear or dislike the police; they may have little confidence in their ability to handle criminal matters or in their willingness to regard citizen complaints as legitimate. Of those who fail to report crimes against them, only a relatively small proportion (3 percent) in the Washington study, failed to do so because of a fear of reprisal. Another small proportion, including businessmen, did not report crimes to the police because they were unwilling to get involved in the criminal-justice system, which they perceived as being time-consuming and offering no personal gain.

There are then significant factors influencing citizens' failure to fulfill their civic obligation to participate in the law-enforcement system. However, primary institutional and organizational relationships within America help to explain this behavior. These relationships are based on con-

4. Albert D. Biderman, et al., *Report on a Pilot Study in the District of Columbia on Victimization and Attitudes toward Law Enforcement,* in President's Commission on Law Enforcement and the Administration of Justice, Field Surveys I (Washington, D.C.: USGPO, 1967), pp. 153–54.

ceptions of personal gain, generally monetary gain or the avoidance of loss in time and effort. The effort is not worth the cost. The institution of insurance looms large in these relationships, since it promises personal gain.

Thus, when citizens call the police, they often are seeking personal gain. The police are expected to protect them, to resolve conflicts in their interest, or to render assistance with a problem. Only a minority of calls request police assistance for others or report crimes where the callers do not personally regard themselves as victimized. Given the absence of a sense of civic responsibility to mobilize the police, and the essentially reactive character of much policing of everyday life, the citizenry has enormous power to subvert the system by its decisions to call the police or not.

Parenthetically, it should be emphasized that citizens possess the capacity to subvert the system of criminal justice in yet other ways. Much depends upon their willingness to cooperate with the police and other agents of criminal justice. How real that subversive capacity is for the system of criminal justice can be seen in our recent studies of the charging process. From the standpoint of the public prosecutor, the decision to make charges depends primarily on the nature of evidence. Given the fact that evidence, more often than not, is verbal testimony of what occurred in social situations, the role of the witness is central to the charging process. When the police serve as the principal witnesses for the state, the subversive capacity lies with them. But with reactive policing, arrest is often by warrant, and the burden of testimony rests with the citizens. Hence, the prosecutor's decision to press charges crucially depends on producing a viable witness, one who will testify for the prosecution and stand up under cross-examination.

This leads us to our first major conclusion: Citizens exercise considerable control over the policing of everyday life through their discretionary decisions to call or not to call the police. That such discretion is also at stake in the policing of collective disorders is clear from the exercise of discretionary authority by present-day college administrators about whether or not to call the police for campus disturbances. At issue, is the question of when is one obligated to call the police, and what are the consequences of citizen discretion for moral order.

Citizen Mobilization of the Police

Because the patrol division of any police department is organized to *react* to citizen requests, it must deal with numerous matters citizens define as police matters. Differences in citizens and police definitions of these matters, and expectations concerning enforcement behavior, often give rise to conflict. Citizens frequently request police intervention in matters which they consider to be of a criminal nature, either because they perceive themselves as victims or they regard the moral order as breached. The police, however, may define these same matters as noncriminal. Even when citizens request assistance both they and the police regard as services (noncriminal matters), there may be disagreement as to what is actually the duty of the police. Police regard it as their duty to find criminals and prevent or solve crimes. The public considers it the duty of the police to respond to its calls and crises: The police should render assistance when citizens request it.

Just how numerous are the noncriminal matters for which citizens mobilize the police can be seen by examining their calls for police assistance. Table 2.1 describes the 6,172 calls received one day in April 1966 at the Central Communications Center of the Chicago Police Department. Complaints about what citizens regard as criminal matters make up 58 percent of all calls to the police. The peace-keeping role of the police is at stake in a substantial proportion of these calls, since 26 percent of all calls report disputes or breaches of the

Table 2.1

Percentage Distribution of a Day's Telephone Communications to
the Chicago Police Department, April 21, 1966 ($n = 6,172$)

Types of communication (Defined by citizens)	Percentage of communications
Request on criminal matters:	
Dispute or breach of peace	26
Offense against property	16
Offense against persons	6
Auto violation	5
Suspicious person	3
Other	2
Subtotal	58
Request for assistance:	
Information	11
Personal/family	9
Medical	8
Traffic accident or hazard	6
Subtotal	34
Complaint about police service:	
Slow police service	2
Unsatisfactory police procedure	1
Subtotal	3
Give police information:	
Missing person	1
Other police matters	4
Subtotal	5
Total	100

SOURCE: Tapes for April 21, 1966, supplied by the Chicago Police
Department. Only calls made to PO5–1212 are included. Calls to
administrative numbers and PAX (the Department's internal telephone system) are excluded.

peace, where the police are expected to restore order. Among
disputes, complaints about juveniles fighting or disturbing
the peace account for 5 in 10 calls, disorderly behavior in
public places 2 in 10, and domestic matters 1 in 10.

Reports of offenses against property accounted for 16 percent of all calls and offenses against persons, 6 percent. Po-

lice regard most of these cases as involving criminal matters. The remainder of complaints considered criminal matters includes complaints about auto violations (5 percent) and reports of suspicious persons (3 percent), with a scattering of complaints about vice, possession of dangerous weapons, and other violations of criminal statutes.

Citizens requested assistance on noncriminal matters in 34 percent of their calls to the police. Their largest demand was for information. Eleven percent of all calls requested information about missing persons, the law, court procedures or appearances, and personal or public matters of importance to the caller, as, for instance, where to get an automobile inspected. Requests for assistance on personal, family, or community problems accounted for 9 percent of all calls. These calls included requests for assistance in finding missing persons, help with animals, and requests to eliminate public hazards. Medical assistance to the sick, injured, or dead accounted for 8 percent of all calls. Reports of traffic hazards and accidents, which were directed to the traffic or accident-investigation division or to the Department of Streets and Public Works, accounted for all other demands for assistance and constituted 6 percent of all calls.

Five percent of all citizen calls offered information to the police. While 1 of every 5 of these calls gave additional information on a matter previously reported by the callers (e.g., further information on a missing person or a crime against them or their property), 4 of every 5 gave information about criminal opportunities and events citizens thought the police should investigate, such as vice or traffic matters. These are matters where the public ordinarily expects the police to act on their own initiative, following a proactive policing policy.

Citizen Preferences and Police Discretion

Often, what citizens regard as criminal matters are processed by the police as noncriminal matters. The discrepancy between citizen mobilization requests on criminal matters and their disposition by the patrol division can be estimated by comparing the April 21 citizen requests for assistance in table 2.1 with the report of incidents handled by the patrol division in Chicago during the 28-day reporting period in April 1966 in table 2.2. Citizens defined 58 percent of all their complaints as criminal matters. The police department dispatched a patrol car in response to almost all of these requests, accounting for 84 percent of all dispatches to the patrol. Yet, during the April reporting period, the patrol division officially processed only 17 percent of all dispatches as criminal incidents.

Crimes against persons such as rape, assault, and robbery made up only 3 percent of all incidents handled by patrol, although they comprised 6 percent of all citizen calls and 9 percent of all dispatches. Burglary and theft made up only 9 percent of all incidents handled by patrol, but they represented 16 percent of all calls and 23 percent of all dispatches. All other crimes totaled 5 percent of incidents handled by patrol, yet they added up to 10 percent of all calls and 18 percent of all dispatches.

More than 8 of every 10 incidents handled by police patrol were regarded by police as noncriminal matters. The police usually treated disputes and disturbances as noncriminal matters while citizens usually considered them criminal matters.

It is interesting to note that disturbances or disputes were present in about equal proportion in citizen requests and police classification, representing respectively 26 percent of all calls and 25 percent of all incidents, yet they represented 38 percent of all dispatches. Assuming these statistics are representative of police dispatches, there is an almost 2 in 5 chance that police officers will have to restore order when they are dispatched to handle complaints from citizens. Since only 6 percent of all disturbances in table 2.2 led to arrest, police intervention depends primarily upon other ways of resolving conflicts. Although the police use physical restraint

Table 2.2

Percentage Distributions for Incidents and Arrests by Arresting Unit of the Patrol Division, Chicago Police Department, March 31 to April 27, 1966

Type of incident	Total incidents in this period	Percentage of all incidents	Total number of arrests	Percentage of arrests from incidents	Percentage of Arrests by: Total	Beat cars	Task force	Other units*
Criminal incidents:								
Serious assault	945	0.7	166	17.6	100	90	2	8
Minor assault	1,550	1.2	266	17.1	100	89	2	9
Armed robbery	693	0.5	50	7.2	100	84	—	16
Strong armed robbery	716	0.6	47	6.6	100	88	11	1
Residential burglary	2,111	1.7	46	2.2	100	93	—	7
Nonresidential burglary	1,307	1.0	136	10.4	100	90	—	10
Motor vehicle theft	2,834	2.2	69	2.4	100	86	6	8
Theft from motor vehicle	897	0.7	14	1.3	100	86	—	14
Theft of motor vehicle accessories	1,217	1.0	11	0.9	100	55	9	36
Purse snatching	322	0.3	12	3.7	100	92	—	8
Bicycle theft	511	0.4	9	1.8	100	89	—	11
Other theft	2,695	2.1	417	15.5	100	95	1	4
Other crimes	5,928	4.6	572	9.6	100	81	4	15
Subtotal	21,726	(17.0)	1,787	(8.2)	100	87	3	10

Table 2.2—Continued

Type of incident	Total incidents in this period	Percentage of all incidents	Total number of arrests	Percentage of arrests from incidents	Percentage of Arrests by:			
					Total	Beat cars	Task force	Other units*
Noncriminal incidents:								
Traffic accident	12,060	9.4	570	4.7	100	96	—	4
Vehicle recovery	1,803	1.4	94	5.2	100	85	5	10
Disturbance	31,548	24.7	1,892	6.0	100	89	†	11
Sick and injured	4,623	3.6	46	1.0	100	17	—	83
Suspicious person	3,954	3.1	114	2.9	100	94	—	6
Miscellaneous	52,147	40.8	2,004	3.8	100	65	†	35
Subtotal	106,135	(83.0)	4,720	4.4	100	79	†	21
Total	127,861	(100.0)	6,507	5.1	100	81	1	18

SOURCE: Patrol Division Operations Report, Chicago Police Department, 4th period, 1966.

*Other units in the districts that are part of patrol include umbrella car, crime car, squadrol, supervising sgts., supervising lts., and local vice units.

†Less than 0.5 percent.

in dealing with some disturbances (other than in sustaining an arrest), conflict resolution must rely primarily on verbal intervention. Verbal intervention includes, of course, threats to use the coercive authority of arrest. Our police observation studies in high-crime-rate areas showed that, in handling disputes, the police tended to rely on negotiated settlements and "cooling out" the participants rather than using coercive authority.[5]

Among noncriminal incidents, emergencies occasioned by traffic accidents and sick and injured calls made up 13 percent of all incidents in table 2.2, upon which police acted, and 14 percent of all citizen calls for service in table 2.1, although they constituted 20 percent of all dispatches. Reports of suspicious persons and situations comprised only 3 percent of all incidents and of all calls.

For the Chicago police, 41 percent of all calls were categorized as miscellaneous incidents, requiring only a brief report. These included civil and private matters which lead to disputes such as those between landlords and tenants or customers and businessmen, requests to locate missing persons, and many minor violations such as motor vehicle standing violations, juveniles playing ball in the street, and sleeping drunks. Less than 4 percent of the miscellaneous incidents led to police citation or arrest. Most of these were simple citations.

The large proportion of noncriminal matters, and particularly, matters which citizens considered of a criminal nature while the police did not, suggests the police exercise enormous discretion in handling citizen calls. It also raises the question of whether the police are arbitrary in labeling these matters, thereby subverting the goals of citizens in mobilizing

5. See Donald J. Black and Albert J. Reiss, Jr., "Patterns of Behavior and Citizen Transactions," in President's Commission on Law Enforcement and the Administration of Justice, *Studies in Crime and Law Enforcement in Major Metropolitan Areas,* Field Surveys III, vol. 2, sec. 1 (Washington, D.C.: USGPO, 1967).

the police. While there is much evidence that the police do exercise enormous discretion, it is far from clear whether their processing and labeling of these matters is arbitrary and controlled solely by them, since there are several reasons why so many citizen calls to the police end up as other than criminal matters.

To begin with, many citizens have only a vague understanding of the difference between civil, private, and criminal matters. They fail to comprehend the legal grounds for police intervention in the affairs of citizens. Much of their ignorance stems from the belief that they are morally right; therefore, the law is on their side and the police should side with them as complainants, disciplining any errant parties. When a citizen, for instance, gets into an argument with a landlord over the payment of rent and the police are called, both the tenant and the landlord may view the action of the other as criminal; each may demand the police take action against the other. A complainant may fail to understand or believe police when he is told the dispute is a civil matter, private legal counsel is advised, it is a matter for the civil courts to resolve, or a purely private matter. Further confusion results when people are aware that the police intervene in *some* landlord-tenant matters, as in the eviction of renters. How can most citizens know when an officer is acting on court orders or on his own, and in the latter case, whether or not he has the authority to do so?

Many incidents citizens regard as criminal must, by law, be handled otherwise, since they do fall into the category of civil or private matters. The police superficially may appear to exercise discretion in civil or private matters, in which citizens and police actually have very little control. Frequently, the police can do little more for citizens who call about these matters than inform them where they may go for additional information or assistance. The failure of police to explain their lack of intervention may only confuse and frustrate citizens further.

It would be wrong to assume that the police handle many matters simply by ignoring them or arbitrating in disputes and disturbances, thus solving the problem, at least temporarily. This form of discretion often makes it unnecessary for citizens to enter these matters into the system of civil law, or bring them to other agencies to handle privately.

Similarly, it cannot be assumed that citizens are without control in such matters. The legal system defines matters as civil or private to protect citizens, thereby granting them, by law, seemingly greater control of such matters. Instead of the "state" pursuing these matters in the state's interest, the citizen is empowered to pursue or defend *his own interests*. Paradoxically, however, this "right" is subverted by the operating system which effectively precludes many citizens from private action, since so much depends upon their ability to arrange and afford legal and other services.

Another reason police receive so many calls of a noncriminal nature is because public and private services are not readily accessible to citizens, and they do not have sufficient information to know where to direct their complaints, particularly when the problem requires attention "now." Citizen demands enter the police system precisely because the police are directly linked to the citizen system at all times, and other appropriate services are not. Police overload with noncriminal matters develops out of the organization's success in making it relatively easy for citizens to penetrate its boundaries with demands for service.

Furthermore, overload results from the fact that the police have come to meet at least some demands for service on noncriminal matters, especially in response to crisis and emergency. Indeed, they often assure citizens that their demands are genuine when there is no effective way to direct the requests to other service agencies.

Departmental policy to dispatch the police in response to all calls, for example, may also increase citizen demand for other kinds of services. If there is no internal provision for meeting the increased demand, overload results. A good illustration of how rapidly overload can develop is shown by the experience of the Detroit Police Department some years ago. Ambulance service for the poor was inadequate in Detroit. Some of the responsibility for meeting this demand for emergency service was shifted to the police department which bought station wagons for beat cars, equipping them for emergency transportation to medical service. Within less than two years, the percentage of "sick runs"—as they came to be known—rose from about 4 percent to 17 percent of all police dispatches. Demand soon outran supply. Many factors determined this large demand for service. What citizens and police regarded as emergency situations soon expanded to cover transportation of the poor to a medical setting for any kind of treatment. This eliminated the dependence of the poor and the aged on public transportation or taxis to take them to medical centers in favor of a faster, more reliable form of transportation by the police.

A third reason why many incidents originally regarded as criminal by citizens are treated as noncriminal or private matters by the police is that the citizen, not the policeman, controls how the incident will be labeled. This fact is easily forgotten by those labeling theorists who grant enormous discretionary power to the police to classify matters citizens bring to their attention. The legal doctrine of probable cause —the police shall make an arrest only when they have reasonable grounds to believe that a crime has been committed —makes the police very dependent upon the citizen in making an arrest.

Often, the only grounds for concluding a crime has been committed is oral testimony. Much of the time, only citizens possess that information, since the crime was committed before the police arrived. Hence, for the police to make an arrest or regard an event as a criminal matter, citizens must agree to cooperate in swearing complaints. Moreover, many matters that could be treated as crimes against persons occur among persons known to one another. A 1960 FBI survey in cities with over 25,000 inhabitants disclosed that in 22 percent of all aggravated assault cases reported by the police, the assailants were members of the same family and in 43 percent, they were neighbors or acquaintances.[6] Similar evidence is available for rapes.[7] Just how important citizen discretion can be in such matters is shown when we examine the clearance rates for Index crimes. An offense may be cleared by an arrest or by exception. Clearance by exception usually means that the police have identified the offender, but elements beyond the control of the police, such as the victim's refusal to prosecute, preclude an arrest. Clearance by exception rates in table 2.3 are above average in Chicago for only two major Index crimes: rape and aggravated assault. It is particularly interesting that, while 28 percent of all aggravated assaults were cleared by arrest, 32 percent were cleared by exception, indicating the unwillingness of citizens to assume responsibility for such arrests. This is the only major Index crime, in fact, where clearance by exception exceeds that of clearance by arrest.

Frequently, in crimes against persons or property where the offenders are known to the complainant, the police are only expected to resolve the crisis in a manner which will preserve the small system of family, friends or acquaintances. Should the police want to make an arrest, the witnesses and complainants "cop out" because of their investments in these small systems. A wife, for example, assumes the risk, in becoming a complainant against her husband, that if arrest and incarceration follow, he will be lost as a breadwinner. The willingness to testify or swear a warrant

6. U.S. Department of Justice, FBI, *Uniform Crime Reports for the United States, 1960* (Washington, D.C.: USGPO, July 24, 1961), p. 11, chart 6.

7. See *Report of the President's Commission on Crime in the District of Columbia* (Washington, D.C.: USGPO, 1966), p. 53; and Menachem Amir, "Patterns in Forcible Rape" (Ph.D. diss., University of Pennsylvania, 1965), p. 496.

Table 2.3

Number and Percentage of Actual Offenses Cleared by the Chicago Police Department,
February 3 to March 2, 1966

Type of complaint or index offense	Number of offenses known to police	Percentage of known offenses			
		Actual*	Cleared† by arrest	Cleared‡ by exception	Not cleared
Total index	7,762	100	11	5	84
Homicide	27	100	89	4	7
Rape	120	100	34	9	57
Robbery	1,302	100	14	1	85
Aggravated assault	759	100	28	32	40
Burglary	2,372	100	8	1	91
Larceny-theft over $50	1,102	100	8	6	86
Auto theft	2,080	100	8	1	91
Total non-index	10,369	100	24	11	65
Total offenses	17,388	100	29	15	56

SOURCE: Special Tabulation, Chicago Police Department, February 3–March 2, 1966.
*For definition of actual offenses, see U.S. Department of Justice, FBI, *Uniform Crime Reporting Handbook* (Washington: USGPO, February, 1965).
†Police clear a crime by arrest "when they have 'identified the offender, have sufficient evidence to charge him and actually take him into custody'" (*Uniform Crime Reports*, 1968, p. 30).
‡A crime is cleared "by exception" when "... some element beyond police control precludes the placing of formal charges against the offender, such as the victim's refusal to prosecute or local prosecution is declined because the subject is being prosecuted elsewhere for a crime committed in another jurisdiction" (*Uniform Crime Reports*, 1968, p. 30).

depends, therefore, upon the cost of jeopardizing personal relations. The arrival of the police often serves to transform an adversary relationship among citizens to one of accommodation. Indeed, at times the problem for the police is to avoid becoming an adversary in such situations. Settlement becomes more an issue of what the adversaries can agree upon and what complainants want, than of what the police can do. When faced with the responsibility to pursue matters as criminal, it is frequently the citizen, not the policeman, who "cops out."

Some criminal matters, particularly those arising between businessmen and citizens or employers and employees are resolved as noncriminal matters, because the complainants have investments in such matters other than in seeing that justice is done. The businessmen, for example, are willing to accept, indeed often want, nothing more than restitution of their financial loss. Just how substantial unofficial handling of crime is for businessmen can be seen from the results of a study for the Small Business Administration on crimes against all United States businesses.[8] When businessmen, who were victims of shoplifting, were asked, "If the police or prosecutor recommends it, would you press charges against a person caught shoplifting in your place of business?" exactly 30 percent said they probably would not. Similar evidence exists for employee theft and customer fraud, as in the passing of bad checks. The main reason businessmen fail to press legal charges for these violations is that business interests depend primarily on financial rather than moral gain. Restitution of the loss is more profitable than prosecution. Moreover, any monetary loss must be balanced against the cost incurred in prosecuting, including time spent pressing charges and in court. Often the complainants calculate that the dollar loss from crime is not worth the cost of doing justice, particularly if the loss is small.

The amount citizens can control the outcome of a transac-

8. For a detailed description of the survey, see Reiss, in *Crime Against Small Business,* pp. 53–143.

tion, which they have reported to the police, is apparent from our observational studies of police and citizen encounters in high-crime-rate areas of three cities. Examining all such encounters where a complainant indicated a preference for police action in the situation, Donald Black discovered that the police tended to act according to the preferences of complainants for police action.[9] Preferences for unofficial handling of a felony or misdemeanor was expressed in about 14 percent of all encounters. The police did not file an official report in a single instance where the complainant expressed a preference for unofficial handling of a felony or misdemeanor. When the complainant expressed a preference for official action by the police, officers tended to follow that preference. The conditions most conducive to officer compliance with a complainant preference for official action occurred when a felony was charged and the suspect was a stranger to the victim; 91 percent of these cases resulted in an official crime report. The police were less likely to adhere to complainant preferences for official action when the incident was a misdemeanor and the suspects were family, friends, neighbors, or acquaintances. This is not surprising, since the police anticipate that many of these complainants will refuse to prosecute when moral indignation passes. An official crime report is least likely when an incident arises between family members, somewhat more likely when it occurs between friends, neighbors, or acquaintances, and most likely when it occurs among strangers with complainant preference controlling police capability for action. Black also found that the more deferential the complainant to the police officer, the more likely the officer was to comply with his request in handling the matter, a further indication that the effect of citizen and police expectations and behavior controls police decisions.[10]

9. See Donald J. Black, "Police Encounters and Social Organization: An Observation Study" (Ph.D. diss., University of Michigan, 1968), pp. 188–92.
10. Ibid., pp. 192–94.

Citizen and Police Enforcement of Law

The way in which citizens mobilize the police to enforce the law depends upon their roles as enforcers of law. For example, a citizen may call the police in the role of victim of crime or, as a witness of a crime against others. He may also complain about criminal opportunities and situations, like gambling, within the community. And, finally, he may complain about the quality and quantity of law enforcement. He may serve as both complainant and informant for the police.

In the majority of calls received by the Chicago Police Department about crime matters, either the victim or a member of his household called the police. In approximately a third of the calls, the citizen who called the police was not a victim of the crime. Citizens may perceive themselves as victims when the public peace is breached even if they are not personally victimized. Our studies of police contacts with residents of high-crime-rate areas, who called the police to report some incident in their neighborhood, showed 56 percent saw themselves as victims, even though, in more than half of these situations, they were not directly and personally victimized. Rather, they reported disturbances in the neighborhood that were annoying, and therefore, in some way directed against them.

The extent to which citizens do not feel obligated to report when they observe another person victimized by a crime is indicative of the degree of anomie in an area. Unfortunately, we lack information on the opportunities citizens have in their daily lives to observe crimes being committed against others, and their discretion to report them to the police when they do. It also cannot be ascertained when citizens know that criminal operations, such as organized crime, exist. Thus, it is difficult to estimate whether citizens more often complain to the police as victims of crime or, in quasi-police roles, as enforcers of the law. We do know that

almost 1 in every 10 residents of high-crime-rate areas reported calling the police to report a crime he observed
being committed, or some minor violation of the municipal
code, or a disturbance in the neighborhood. Moreover, when
all calls from people in these neighborhoods are considered,
more than 4 in 10 concerned matters where the citizens
were not directly involved as victims. At least, in these cases,
citizens are fulfilling a civic obligation to help others and
call the police.

Citizen complaints about the quality of police service
may account for significant input into a police department.
Surprisingly, 3 percent of all April 21 calls to the Chicago
Police in table 2.1 registered complaints about police service, a matter we shall turn to later.

There is some difficulty distinguishing the citizen role as
informant from that of complainant. Of all citizen calls to
the Chicago Police in table 2.1, 4 percent gave the police
information about crime situations or opportunities. The
frequency of such calls by citizens—as many as 250 in a
single day in Chicago—is undoubtedly a function of department policy. The Chicago police encourage citizens to
be "tipsters." Citizens therefore call and write to the police
department about matters they consider criminal. Although
some citizens may identify themselves in such communications to the department, many choose to remain anonymous.

Superintendent O. W. Wilson of the Chicago Police Department permitted me to examine their anonymous complainant file for the first three 28–day reporting periods of
1964. This is the only record of information on anonymous
tips and complaints to the police of which I am aware. There
were only 106 written tips compared with an estimated
7,000 telephone tips during the same period.

According to crime tips obtained from anonymous letters
to Superintendent Wilson (see table 2.4), it is surprising that
almost 3 of every 4 deal with vice activity ordinarily associated with organized crime: bookmaking and gambling,

Table 2.4

Percentage Distribution of Citizen's Complaints in 106 Anonymous
Letters to the Superintendent of Police of the Chicago Police
Department, January 1 to March 16, 1964   .

Type of complaint	Percentage
Liquor sales to minors	12
Violation of liquor laws	6
Predatory juvenile gangs	6
Gambling and bookmaking	37
Prostitution	15
Narcotics and dope traffic	9
Extortion (juice and shakedowns)	7
B-girls	6
Homosexual bars or activity	2

SOURCE: Special Tabulation, Chicago Police Department, 1964.

prostitution and B-girls, narcotics and other drug traffic,
and extortion. Violations of liquor laws accounted for 18
percent of the tips, with sales to minors the more frequent
complaint. Two percent of the tips were about gay bars or
homosexual activity. More than 9 of every 10 letters to the
chief of police complained about businesses or their op-
erators who sell goods and services where moral matters
are at issue. There were no anonymous complaints about
fellow citizens who engaged in such moral violations, nor,
for that matter, in any other crime.

Most anonymous letters to the chief are written by
women. They complain usually in the role of offended wife
or concerned mother. As mothers, they complain that their
children are being victimized by predatory juvenile gangs,
are being sold liquor when underage, or are becoming ad-
dicted to narcotics. As wives, they complain about husbands
being cheated by gamblers or prostitutes. Perhaps their
anonymity in writing to the police stems from their roles of
wife or mother, where they do not wish those close to them
to know they have complained.

Among the male complainants, three types emerge. The

first is the moral entrepreneur, usually a clergyman, who demands a clamp down on gambling, prostitution, homosexuality, or narcotics traffic in his community. He specifically names establishments police should close or vice lords whom they should arrest. The second type is the businessman who, to operate a legitimate enterprise, must make payoffs to the syndicate or who, unable to secure conventional loans, must turn to the syndicate, thus becoming a victim of the "juice racket." Fearing reprisal from the underworld if personally identified as a complainant, he seeks relief through the anonymous complaint. And, third, is the stranger to the city who frequents bars where he is cheated or robbed by that special class of waitresses who "push drunks" and are known as B-girls. Or else, in seeking a prostitute, he is either cheated by the "Murphy" game where he pays but receives no service, or is robbed and assaulted by the prostitute's accomplice or pimp. Fearing public degradation or private recrimination from those close to him if he identifies himself as a victim to the police, he chooses to remain anonymous in his complaint.

Almost all citizens who wrote these anonymous letters to the chief demanded the police pursue a more proactive policy in policing the morals of the city. They regarded it as the bounden duty of the police to control as well as eliminate the businesses. In most cases, they requested immediate action against the violators. However, by choosing anonymity, they abdicated the role of a complainant, who may assist the police by identifying the actual victim or victims—who might then, themselves, serve as complainants. This abdication of civic responsibility means the police must take a proactive vice role if legal action is to follow. Parenthetically, it might be noted that much seemingly proactive policing of vice by morals squads of a police department are reactions to these anonymous complaints.

Perhaps the reason citizens write the chief about vice matters is that they see themselves as victimized by the failure of the police to eliminate vice in the community. This basis for notifying the police about crime opportunities in the city contrasts sharply with the basis for citizens making tips, particularly when they identify themselves. Generally, when a citizen provides tips, he regards himself as an informant rather than a victim. Informants appear to derive vicarious satisfaction from acting in a crime-detection role, a role of the police.

I have tried to show the principal ways citizens exercise control over the inputs into a law-enforcement system. They have considerable influence over what becomes a police matter and what is processed as crime, based on their decisions to mobilize the police or not, their demands and complaints for police intervention, their preferences for arrest, and their willingness to aid the police as complainants.

Police Organization and Discretion over Inputs

Citizen and police initiative create almost all the input into police departments that is processed in the system of criminal justice. Only a very small proportion of input derives from such other sources as warrants issued on the initiative of the prosecutor or the bench, or information from other police agencies. We have termed the police force a reactive organization when it is mobilized by calls or complaints from citizens, and a proactive organization when it seeks criminal violations on its own initiative. But, what are the effects of proactive and reactive organization on police discretion?

The public typically regards the police as proactive in their work, a view shared by some students of police organization.[11] The detective and traffic divisions, the specialized vice and organized crime bureaus, the task force, even patrol, are regarded as proactive units of the depart-

11. Jerome Skolnick, *Justice without Trial* (New York: John Wiley, 1966).

ment. The public's views on policing may be molded more by their perceptions of what police do when they come into contact with citizens (such as questioning, directing traffic, searching people and their property), than by an understanding of how they happen to come into contact with them.

The intake process in large metropolitan police departments is organized around divisions and bureaus. From the standpoint of the police departments, it is wrong to consider such units or the police roles in them, such as detective or patrolman, as proactive in nature. The major divisions of a police department usually engage in both proactive and reactive police work. Although the traffic division may have major responsibility for policing motor vehicle standing and moving violations, traffic officers also may respond to commands from central communications to investigate automobile accidents and traffic hazards particularly if there is no specialized automobile accident investigation bureau. Moreover, much of the work of the division is to control the flow of traffic, an activity that is a reaction to predictable patterns of vehicle movement. Indeed, to control traffic often entails ignoring moving violations or shouting at violators rather than impeding vehicle movement by making an arrest.

The detective division would seem to be *the* proactive division of the department. Yet much of its work is not of this nature. Detectives generally investigate incidents already reported by citizens and investigated by patrolmen. They may be assigned the major task of determining whether or not the crime reported by the citizen is bona fide or unfounded. When bona fide, the role of the detective may be limited to locating and arresting the citizen listed in the complaint. At most, the detective division's proactive work is limited to solving known crimes by finding violators. Even when detectives or plainclothes men (in vice squads) appear to discover violations and violators on their own initiative, the seemingly planned investigations often are precipitated by information or complaints received from citizens.

Similarly, the patrol division of any major police department is organized both to investigate complaints from citizens through dispatch from a central command and to do preventive patrol. For example, a patrolman may be dispatched, by a citizen call, to investigate a suspicious situation or a suspicious person, he may be stopped by a citizen while on routine patrol, or he may investigate entirely on his own initiative.

Crime prevention is a general goal for most police departments and they are organized to deal with the problem from different angles. The public information and education bureaus utilize various informational and educational techniques to get businesses, citizens, or specialized publics (e.g. school children), to adopt crime prevention or safety practices. The detective division may provide assistance to employers screening job applicants. The task force, or some specialized vice or crime unit, may be assigned to public events to prevent the theft that is prevalent on such occasions. The patrol division generally assumes that, when an officer is not in service handling matters assigned to him, he is engaged in routine preventive work.

Most of the time, officers are on routine or beat patrol, on foot or in a car. In this capacity, they are not usually working to reduce a specific type of crime, although routine door checks of business places may be considered a preventive measure. Other than providing information and education or displaying visible signs of police authority, such as patrolling, most police techniques of crime prevention are not specific to preventing crime. Rather, they are general techniques commonly used by the police for detection and verification that crimes have been committed. Thus, wiretapping, interrogation, and search of the person can occur with or without probable cause. Their use in preventive work depends upon the officer's judgment of behavior, motivation, and situation. Moreover, some techniques of prevention are closely entwined with methods for detecting violations. Speed traps, for example, are designed to prevent violation of speed limits by detecting violators. Frequently, success of these preventive measures is evaluated in terms of the number of violators apprehended rather than in terms of what is prevented. The latter can be evaluated by measuring the growth or reduction in the rate of violation or violative behavior, as, for example, a decline in the rate of assault. Similarly, the effect of searching persons may be assessed in terms of how many arrests are made of persons found carrying dangerous weapons or narcotics —crimes of possession—rather than in how much such crime is reduced.

In pursuit of its aim to protect citizens, preventive work often requires intervention in the lives of some citizens on the initiative of the police. The core of much of this work is the investigation of the suspicious person and the suspicious situation by traditional techniques of police intervention.

Most preventive techniques do not produce much input into the system of criminal justice. Police departments, therefore, do not require that an official record be kept of the use of such techniques. The problem of producing an official production statistic of crime prevention creates certain dilemmas for police administrators. To the degree that success is measured in terms of arrests for crimes, the official crime rate of a department often rises rather than falls due to increased police activity. Citizens, with their simple notions of crime prevention, might expect it to decline. And, to the degree that the department reports how unproductive any technique of crime prevention is in terms of arrests, it risks charges either of poor police performance or of unnecessary intervention in the lives of citizens. Given the great difficulty in measuring crimes prevented, departments tend to pin their programs of prevention on demonstrating how a falling crime rate follows major efforts at prevention.

Preventive investigation or patrol originates both with

citizens and the police. Which group contributes most to
preventive activity depends upon policies of the department
and practices of citizens and the police. Where citizens are
encouraged to report matters of potential crime to the
police, as they were in Chicago during Superintendent Wilson's administration, the volume of such calls is substantial.
Of the calls made to the Chicago Police Department on
April 21 (table 2.1), 3 percent were requests to investigate
suspicious persons or situations. Where the police department organizes units of preventive policing of everyday life,
as does the New Orleans Police Department, the extent of
such activity is substantial.

Statistics for the New Orleans Police Department for
1967 report pedestrian and residence checks by the tactical
unit and the canine corps. The tactical unit made 30,148
pedestrian checks and 947 juvenile checks. They made, in
addition, 42,641 checks of business places and 13,185
checks of vehicles, some of which undoubtedly involved
contact with citizens. Considering only the combined 31,095
checks of pedestrians and juveniles, the police made 5,397
arrests, for an arrest rate of 17.4 percent. Similarly, during
1967, the canine corps checked 7,770 pedestrians, 389
suspicious persons, and 1,121 juveniles, making a total of
882 arrests, for a somewhat lower arrest rate of 9.5 percent.
An unknown proportion of these checks was made with
prior knowledge of which person to check, so they are not
all strict examples of proactive policing. Nonetheless, the
statistics disclose a substantial volume of proactive policing
by these units.

From April 15 to December 31, these units with the
patrol division reported 47,834 stops of citizens of whom
25,230 were frisked, resulting in a frisk rate of 53 percent
and an arrest rate of 17 percent. The 25,230 frisks yielded
only 113 weapons, creating a weapons-productivity rate of
less than half of 1 percent.

In 1967, the Communication Center of the New Orleans

Police Department reported receiving 259,462 complaints. If we compare this figure with the estimated 107,241 stops or checks of citizens by police in 1967, we arrive at a police input rate that is 41 percent, that of citizen mobilizations of the police. This estimated rate of police input is undoubtedly low, since we lack information on proactive contacts of officers assigned to other department units, as in the cases of vice and narcotic plainclothes men. There may also be considerable underreporting by all officers for such proactive techniques as search of the person. Thus, the volume of proactive policing in New Orleans, excluding traffic policing, may easily be half that of reactive mobilizations. On balance, nevertheless, the mobilization of the police appears to rest more with citizens than it does with officers, even where proactive policing is highly legitimated by police authorities as is the case in New Orleans.

Our observations of the policing of everyday life in the high-crime-rate precincts of Boston, Chicago, and Washington, D.C. indicated that the probability a suspect would be searched was 1 in 5 in both dispatched and on-view mobilizations in each of the cities, a rate far below that of New Orleans. Further, these searches—in both on-view and dispatched encounters—revealed 1 in 10 whites and 1 in 4 Negroes possessed a gun, knife, or other dangerous weapon.[12] Searches of the person in these cities yielded considerably more dangerous weapons than New Orleans. How can we account for such differences from city to city? The fact that the statistics are city-wide for New Orleans and only pertain to high-crime-rate precincts in the other cities may account for some of the difference. Another important factor, here, may be differences in the exercise of discretionary authority. Searches in Boston, Chicago, and Washington, were usually conducted only when there were reasonable grounds to believe a crime had been committed. By con-

12. See Black and Reiss, "Patterns of Behavior in Police and Citizen Transactions," pp. 80–94.

trast, stop and frisk practices, as used in New Orleans, often are based more on preceptions of suspicious behavior than on probable cause, permitting much wider latitude in the exercise of discretion.

The effectiveness of the discretion exercised by officers in proactive versus reactive patrol can be crudely measured by comparing the results of on-view mobilizations with citizen mobilizations of the police. Unfortunately the on-view official statistics compiled by police departments include matters that citizens bring to the attention of the police when out on patrol, as well as those the police seek out on their own initiative. Nevertheless, these official statistics permit us to compare the effectiveness of preventive and dispatched patrols. "Crimes known to the police" is used as the measure of productivity on the assumption that when the police are on routine preventive patrol of everyday life, crimes will be uncovered either because citizens bring them to police attention or because police encounter them "in progress."

Some data for the city of Chicago permit us to compare the productivity of preventive and dispatched patrol. Returning to the city-wide data for Chicago for the fourth-reporting period of 1966, there were 1,121 beat cars assigned to routine patrol during this period. Although not all of these cars were in service for all shifts of the 28-day period, we are assuming they were for purposes of estimation. Allowing routine lunch or rest breaks, we estimate a car to be in service on patrol duty 22 hours each day. For the 1,021 beat cars, this amounts to 22,462 hours in service each day or an estimated 628,391 car hours for the 28-day period. More man than car hours were required for patrol, since two men were assigned to 384 of the beat cars. Daily man hours on patrol duty in Chicago during this period accordingly amounted to an estimated 865,480 hours during the 28-day period.

The patrol division reported an average of 62 minutes

in service to handle each criminal incident and 39 minutes
for each noncriminal incident during this 28-day period.
Crude estimates were made of the man hours spent by
patrol in handling dispatched and on-view encounters
during the period using these average times. We estimate
that, of the total hours cars were assigned to duty, only 14
percent of the time was spent on dispatch, leaving 86 percent for routine preventive patrol. Actually, less than 1 percent of the time officers are on patrol is spent handling
on-view matters. And, only 1 percent of the time on routine
preventive patrol is spent in handling criminal and noncriminal incidents (table 2.5). Overall, 99 percent of the
time in preventive patrol nets no criminal or noncriminal
incidents, an indication that preventive patrol is markedly
unproductive of police matters processed in the system of
criminal justice.

Table 2.5

Estimated Hours Spent by Beat Cars on Major Types of Patrol Activity by the
Chicago Police Department, March 31 to April 27, 1966

Allocation of beat car by activity	Total car hours	Percentage by activity	Percentage of inservice	Percentage of preventive patrol
ɔatched subtotal	(87,957)	(14)	(94)	—
ʻriminal incident	18,108	3	19	—
ʻoncriminal incident	69,849	11	75	—
ʋiew subtotal	(5,334)	(1)	(6)	1
ʼriminal incident	999	0.1	1	0.2
Noncriminal incident	4,335	0.7	5	0.8
service subtotal	(93,291)	(15)	100	—
ıtine patrol	535,100	85	—	99
ventive subtotal	(540,434)	(86)	—	100
Total activity	628,391	100	—	—

SOURCE: Patrol Division Operations Report, Chicago Police Department, 4th
Period, 1966.

Even more striking is the low productivity of preventive patrol for criminal matters alone, since only about two-tenths of 1 percent of the time spent on preventive patrol is occupied in handling criminal matters. What is more, only 3 percent of all time spent on patrol involves handling what is officially regarded as a criminal matter. Considering only the time spent in service, a mere 20 percent is spent in handling criminal matters (table 2.5).

The results are equally striking when we examine the incidents, which constitute the raw material for the criminal-

Table 2.6

Percentage Distribution of 127,861 Incidents Handled by the Patrol Division of the Chicago Police Department, March 31 to April 27, 1966

Type of unit and type of incident	All incidents	Type of mobilization	
		Dispatch ("on call")	On view
Total police activity	100.0	93.1	6.9
Criminal incidents only	17.0	16.0	1.0
Noncriminal incidents only	83.0	77.1	5.9
Beat cars in their own beats			
Criminal incidents	4.6	4.4	0.2
Noncriminal incidents	18.4	17.1	1.3
Beat cars in other beats of district			
Criminal incidents	10.3	9.7	0.6
Noncriminal incidents	39.7	37.6	2.1
Other district units in district			
Criminal incidents	0.3	0.2	0.1
Noncriminal incidents	12.7	11.4	1.3
Task force units in district			
Criminal incidents	*	*	*
Noncriminal incidents	*	*	*
Other department units in district			
Criminal incidents	1.7	1.6	0.1
Noncriminal incidents	12.3	11.1	1.2

SOURCE: Patrol Division Operations Report, Chicago Police Department, 4th period, 1966.
*Less than 0.5 percent

justice system (table 2.6). About 93 percent of all incidents processed by the patrol division in Chicago developed from citizen initiative. Of all dispatched and on-view incidents handled by the Chicago police, only 17 percent involved criminal matters, and most of these originated from citizen calls to the police. Only 1 percent of all incidents originated in on-view settings.

Some people may regard these findings as evidence that the mobile patrol is a poor means of preventive patrol and ineffective in seeking out criminal matters that are processed in the criminal-justice system. They may claim that, in the past, when police were organized around the foot patrol, they were far more effective in dealing with crime. However, such an attitude may rest in nostalgia rather than fact. There is good reason to believe that the foot patrolman responded primarily to citizen mobilizations, he was relatively ineffective in dealing with crimes without citizen cooperation, he rarely discovered crimes in progress, and his capacity to prevent any crime was extremely limited by his restricted mobility, especially after the advent of the automobile.

The organization of modern police departments around a mobile patrol also may be based on questionable assumptions about its capacity to deal with crime on a territorial basis. Most centralized police commands assign the same men to the same beat or territory for an extended period of time. Moreover, the practice is to respond to a citizen call for assistance by dispatching the beat car regularly assigned to the territory where the request is made, if that car is available at the time of the call.

It is assumed that assignment on this basis costs the department less on the average in time, travel, and manpower, and police administrators believe that the reduction in time it takes to respond to a citizen's call for assistance not only satisfies the citizen, but also optimizes the likelihood police will arrive in time to catch violators or prevent more serious crimes from occurring. They also believe that officers, assigned to an area on a regular basis, will possess considerable intelligence on the people living in it, and this will make them more effective in policing everyday life and preventing crime.

These administrative assumptions are open to question. The population in an area is often so large that no officer can know more than a very small proportion of its members, even granting he is able to get in contact with them. And then, the high rate of mobility in urban populations—at least 1 in 5 changes his place of residence each year—similarly renders such knowledge less useful. One can find other bases for questioning whether officers regularly assigned to an area can do more than establish contact with the most visible segments of that population. In fact, it is not clear that even current, more sophisticated police operations can effectively handle such assignments, given the organization of the modern command and control center of a police department. Let us, therefore, examine how the dispatch process works in a modernized police department such as Chicago.

The system problem is to assign a limited number of police cars to respond to as many legitimate calls for police service as possible within the shortest time. Given the considerable daily, weekly, and even seasonal variation in volume, this is not easy. Yet, an important safety valve exists for the system in the form of preventive patrol. Since much of the time cars are not in service but on routine patrol with no specific duty, it makes the problem of matching beat cars to citizen calls simpler. The dispatcher, in response to a citizen call, routinely dispatches the beat car assigned to the territory where the incident is to be investigated or a report made. When that particular beat car is already in service, the practice is to select another car closest to the destination of the dispatch and not in service.

Let us consider how this procedure works out in a modern police department such as Chicago's where, as already noted, cars are in service only about 15 percent of the time. In the fourth reporting period for patrol operations in Chicago in 1966, we observe that fewer than one-third of all criminal incidents were handled by beat cars in their own beat. Only a little more than one-fourth of all criminal incidents originating from dispatches were handled by patrolmen within their own beat. Many police administrators regard a patrolman's intelligence on a community to be of most importance in noncriminal matters, where an officer must exercise the greatest degree of discretion. However, despite this, officers in Chicago handled an even smaller proportion of all noncriminal incidents, arising from dispatches to their own beat, than criminal incidents. Since routine patrol generally takes place in an officer's own beat, we would expect these officers to deal with a disproportionate number of on-view matters, particularly those connected with preventive patrol. But, even that was not the case in Chicago, where beat cars handled only one-third of all incidents, and one-fifth of all criminal incidents arising on their own beats. The results were the same for noncriminal matters in on-view situations.

Based on these Chicago data, it appears conclusive that beat cars, whether dispatched or on routine preventive patrol, are more likely to handle incidents outside their own area than within it. This fact sharply contradicts the reasonable assumption that officers would spend more time in routine preventive patrol within their own beat than outside of it. This problem may actually be due to the fact that beat cars are dispatched to handle incidents outside their beat. Once a car is dispatched to handle a call outside its beat, the probability of its handling outside calls increases, since, while that car is in service, any call to its beat must be assigned to a car from a neighboring beat. Calls to that beat in turn must be handled by a neighboring car. The problem of such chain effects is a familiar one in systems analysis.

Short of providing reserve manpower in every beat to handle close to the maximum volume generated in that beat, or adopting a queuing method of selective response, the likelihood is slight that, in a centralized command with a dispersed force, an officer can deal with most of the incidents in his own territory. These facts say more, however. Though actual probabilities are lacking, the likelihood that an officer or his car will be present when any crime occurs must be extremely low, particularly since the occurrence of crime is so unpredictable.

These facts show that police on preventive patrol handle little in the way of criminal matters, that they are less likely to do so within their own beat than outside of it, and that they are very unlikely to be present when crimes or other incidents occur. This casts serious doubt on any model of proactive crime control for the policing of everyday life that is based on the distribution of police manpower to handle incidents as they may arise in the presence of the police. Indeed, the data support the view that, to police everyday life by mobile patrol, the patrol must be organized to react to citizen requests for service, allowing the citizen to control inputs into the system of criminal justice.

This is supported further by an examination of the productivity of some of the most highly proactive units of the patrol division or task force. The task force of the Chicago Police Department surprisingly generates very few criminal or noncriminal incidents (table 2.6). In fact, it generated more inputs when it was dispatched than from its own initiative on patrol. Similarly, other units of the patrol division in Chicago (supervision, squadrol, crime cars, and special investigative units assigned to the precinct commander) are more likely to handle matters arising from dispatch rather than on-view policing, and their rate of productivity per unit also is very low (table 2.6).

One is led to question how productive proactive policing can actually be in the United States, since it is clear that this method depends so heavily on reactive forms of organization (where citizen calls or complaints are the major source of inputs on criminal matters). Stinchcombe has pointed out that the legal institutions of privacy, limiting police access to private places, tend to hinder the police in developing and processing criminal matters.[13] The protection of the private place, he maintains, limits the proactive capacity of the police to investigate places where they might discover criminal matters.

Institutions of privacy doubtlessly affect police practice. Not only do they protect the integrity of private places from ready access by the police, but they also protect the integrity of individuals in public through such guarantees as citizen rights before police interrogation, surveillance, or search of the person. They also affect the manner of investigation that takes place following the discovery of a crime and the procuring of evidence to meet the criteria for admissibility in courts of law. These limitations on police access to private places make the police particularly dependent upon the organization of access to them on a reactive basis, using calls to private places as the major basis for entering them. I, personally, do not believe that these institutions of privacy are responsible for the essentially reactive character of policing of private places. The character of policing, whether proactive or reactive, is, to a great extent, determined by the way in which knowledge of a crime is acquired or by the predictability of its occurrence. We noted earlier that proactive patrol generates little volume of criminal matters in public places. In instances where the time and place of a crime cannot be forecast and the frequency of its occurrence in any one place is low, it makes little difference whether that crime occurs in a public or private place. Police access to public parks, for example, has not been particularly effective in discovering crimes within them.

In the absence of massive police manpower, proactive policing is a feasible method for discovery only when crime is

13. Arthur L. Stinchcombe, "Institutions of Privacy in the Determination of Police Administrative Practice," *The American Journal of Sociology* 69 (September 1963): 158.

routine and organized, and therefore predictable. From a sociological point of view, the patterned activity of vice, traffic, and organized groups such as gangs, lend themselves to proactive forms of policing, and therefore to specialized units of police organization and tactics. Proactive policing is the province of specialized units such as narcotics or morals squads, where one can intervene in transactions that are part of an organized system of transactions.

Again, any limitations on the organization of proactive policing, whether institutional or organizational shift the policing of everyday life to reactive forms. Yet, it does not follow altogether that the effectiveness of reactive policing depends much more than the effectiveness of proactive policing on the willingness of the citizenry to comply with police enforcement of the law. The role of citizen cooperation in both forms cannot be minimized.

Dependence of Police Departments
on Reactive Organization

It is difficult to measure the degree to which American municipal police depend upon citizens to police everyday life and to process criminal matters to the point where the police may arrest citizens for violations of the law. The facts presented thus far show that what often appears to be police discretion in making decisions to process matters as criminal or noncriminal is actually based on citizen discretion.

The major inputs into the criminal-justice system examined here are arrests of citizens. These are the only reasonably commensurable data with which we can compare the major divisions of a police department. The 1965 arrest data for Washington, D.C. were chosen to illustrate the degree to which proactive and reactive units of a department account for arrests. Arrests for Part I and Part II offenses are reported in table 2.7 for the major divisions of Washington's

Table 2.7

Percentage Distribution of Arrests by Police Division and Part I Offense Charged for Washington, D.C., 1965

Part I offense class	Police division						Total percentage	Total number
	Patrol division	Canine division	Morals division	Detective division	Traffic division	All others†		
Criminal homicide	65	*	0	21	13	*	100	189
Rape and attempted rape	50	*	0	39	9	2	100	183
Robbery and attempted robbery	77	2	0	19	1	1	100	1,863
Aggravated assault	95	1	*	3	*	1	100	2,811
Burglary and attempted burglary	93	1	*	5	*	1	100	2,553
Larceny—theft	90	1	*	4	1	3	100	4,083
Auto theft	67	3	*	26	2	1	100	1,380
Total, Part I offenses	87	2	*	9	1	1	100	13,062

SOURCE: *Annual Report of the Metropolitan Police Department of Washington, D.C., Fiscal Year, 1965*, p. 38.
*Less than 0.5 percent.
†Includes harbor patrol (7 charges) and youth-aid division (184 charges).

Metropolitan Police Department.[14] These divisions are patrol, canine, morals, detective, and traffic. The harbor and youth-aid divisions handled only a small number of offenses.

For all 1965 Part I offenses in table 2.7, 87 percent of the arrests were made by patrol division. Most of the complaints prompting these arrests undoubtedly arose from citizen calls to the police, since our observations of patrol in four high-crime-rate precincts in Washington, D.C. showed that almost no criminal incidents arose from on-view policing by the patrol. Only the detective division, which made 9 percent of all arrests, contributed much to the volume of Part I arrests. Actually, patrol made 9 of every 10 arrests for the offenses of aggravated assault, burglary and attempted burglary, and larceny-theft. The detective division accounted for one-fifth of the arrests for criminal homicide, and robbery and attempted robbery; one-fourth for auto theft; and two-fifths for rape and atempted rape, offenses where investigation following report of the offense is most likely to result in an arrest. These are also offenses where victims or other persons readily supply information that helps to identify a suspect, in many cases even telling who he is. The traffic division accounted for only about 10 percent of the arrests for criminal homicide, and rape and attempted rape, the investigations of which produced charges. Charges for homicides handled by the traffic division usually arise from automobile accident investigations.

The striking fact in table 2.7 is that the patrol division accounted for no less than 50 percent of the arrests for any Part I offense. Excluding rape and attempted rape, the patrol division acounts for at least two-thirds of all arrests for any offense. A major reason for this is that, in the aggregate, arrests do not result from investigation by a specialized divi-

14. *Annual Report of the Metropolitan Police Department Washington, D.C.*, Fiscal Year, 1965. Part I and Part II offenses are defined in U.S. Department of Justice, FBI, *Uniform Crime Reporting Handbook,* (Washington, D.C.: USGPO, February, 1965).

sion of the department, such as the detective division, but rather from the routine activity of patrol as it responds to citizen calls for assistance.

Citizens contribute most substantially to the arrest of other citizens as violators for several reasons. The police solve many crimes by arrest simply because they have been mobilized by citizens to the location of an incident; the suspect is present and can be easily arrested. The citizen identifies the violator for the patrolman who then takes charge and is officially credited with the arrest. Moreover, the capacity of the police to solve any crime is severely limited by citizens, partly owing to the fact that there is no feasible way to solve most crimes except by securing the cooperation of citizens to link a person to the crime. Finally, the investigation of crimes to locate a violator is expensive. Even if most crimes were solvable, in the sense of finding the persons who committed them (which they are not), the average cost of solving a crime would be beyond the capacity of the citizenry to afford it.

When Part II offenses are considered in table 2.8, the distinctive functions of each of the major divisions of a police department become apparent. The dominance of the patrol division in making arrests is even greater for Part II offenses than for Part I offenses. In fact, most of the arrests for Part II offenses in table 2.8 (excluding motor vehicle violations) were made by the patrol division. It made, for example, almost all arrests for drunkenness, disorderly conduct, minor assaults, vandalism, weapons offenses, and those classified as "all other offenses." The Washington, D.C. patrol also leads in issuing traffic citations or making arrests in traffic matters; more than 6 of every 10 citations for violations were written by the patrol division, a consequence of assigning ticket quotas to officers on patrol for both moving and standing violations.

Table 2.8 also makes clear the specialized functions of the morals, detective, and traffic divisions. Except for vice of-

Table 2.8

Percentage Distribution of Arrests by Police Division and Charges for Part II Offenses in the District of Columbia, 1965

Part II offense class	Police division						Total percentage	Total number
	Patrol division	Canine division	Morals division	Detective division	Traffic division	All others†		
Other assaults	93	1	1	1	*	4	100	2,205
Arson	76	—	—	21	—	3	100	33
Forgery and counterfeiting	51	1	—	46	1	*	99	285
Fraud	34	—	*	64	1	—	99	464
Embezzlement	57	—	—	43	—	—	100	105
Stolen property	82	3	2	9	3	2	101	203
Vandalism	91	4	*	3	*	1	99	1,160
Weapon offense	91	2	1	3	1	1	99	1,784
Prostitution	39	*	61	—	—	—	100	226
Sex offense	45	—	45	10	*	*	100	458
Drug-law violation	26	1	72	1	*	*	100	902
Gambling	63	—	36	*	*	*	99	1,491
Offenses against family	55	2	—	2	2	39	100	51
Driving while intoxicated	63	—	—	—	37	—	100	256

Table 2.8—Continued

Part II offense class	Police division						Total percentage	Total number
	Patrol division	Canine division	Morals division	Detective division	Traffic division	All others†		
Liquor-law violation	74	—	25	*	—	*	100	1,964
Drunkenness	98	1	*	*	1	*	100	44,792
Disorderly conduct	95	2	1	1	1	*	100	20,446
Vagrancy	88	—	10	1	*	1	100	892
All other Part II offenses	95	1	*	2	1	1	100	7,953
Fugitive from justice	54	*	*	23	2	20	99	1,577
Road and driving violations	60	1	*	*	39	*	100	94,678
Parking violations	64	—	—	—	36	—	100	333,642
Traffic and motor-vehicle law violations	73	*	*	*	27	*	100	18,173
Total part II offenses	68	*	1	*	31	*	100	533,740
Total traffic offenses	63	*	*	*	37	*	100	446,493
Total part II offenses, less traffic	93	1	3	2	1	*	100	87,247
Total part I and part II offenses	68	*	*	1	30	*	99	546,802
Total part I and part II offenses, less traffic	92	1	2	3	1	1	100	100,309

SOURCE: *Annual Report of the Metropolitan Police Department of Washington, D.C.*, Fiscal Year, 1965, p. 39.

*Less than 0.5 percent.

†This includes harbor patrol (59 charges); youth-aid division (842 charges); and AH & CR (23 charges).

fenses, the morals division produced very few arrests for any major offenses or Part II offenses. It accounted for 7 of every 10 arrests for violations of narcotics laws, 6 of 10 for prostitution, roughly 4 of 10 for sex offenses and gambling, and 1 of 4 for liquor-law violations. The only other area where the morals division accounted for many arrests was vagrancy, where it made 1 in 10 arrests. The charge of vagrancy in these cases was most likely a cover or substitute charge for some other morals offense.

The detective division dominates in arrests for crimes where there are clear leads to investigation, particularly crimes where citizens provide information that permits ready identification of the offender. As already noted, detectives accounted for 4 of every 10 arrests for rape or attempted rape. In many of these cases, victims already knew the offender before the offense was committed. The same is true for criminal homicide, and to a lesser degree for robbery.[15] Detectives also account for a substantial proportion of arrests for crimes against businesses—fraud, embezzlement, and forgery—in which businessmen often know the offender who must be located. Almost by definition, the offender is not present when the police are notified of the crime's occurrence. What is more, there is reason to believe that businessmen do not notify the police of the offense unless they have reason to know the offender can be located. They are more interested in recovering their loss than in convicting the offender. The only other offenses for which detectives accounted for at least 2 in every 10 arrests were arson and fugitives from justice, again, offenses where knowledge of offenders pays off in leads to arrest.

There is a paradoxical relationship between the way in which detective work is organized to solve crimes and how crimes are actually solved by arrest. Police departments ideally organize detective divisions to solve those crimes that

15. *Uniform Crime Reports,* 1965, pp. 6–11.

require intensive investigation. Yet, we maintain that most of the knowledge that contributes to solution through investigation is based on citizen information on the identity of the suspects. Detective investigation more often depends upon *locating* a known offender than in following leads to deduce the identity of an offender. The media view of the detective, epitomized by Sherlock Holmes, James Bond, or Joe Friday, hardly squares with the reality of most detective work that leads to an arrest. This is not to say that detectives don't follow the ideal model, investigating many crimes that do not lead to arrest, but rather, their role in producing arrests is far more restricted than the ideal model implies.

Based on this description of the detective division, we are led to question the capacity of detectives to solve most crimes through induction and reasoning from evidence, although the importance of such a division in securing convictions is great. To cast doubt on the capacity of detectives to solve crimes is not to question their merit in the production of evidence. The detective division must develop and assemble evidence to meet the legal criteria for its introduction into trial proceedings. In a legal system where procedural matters often are more important than substantive questions, the evidence-producing role of the detective is crucial. Crimes are often more easily solved based on criteria of arrest than on criteria for conviction. The police exercise more control over the former than the latter.

Despite the existence of a youth division in many large police departments, its role in the production of juvenile offenders is generally negligible. Again, that function, for the most part, depends on citizen mobilization of the patrol division to respond to offenses committed by juveniles (table 2.9). The youth division, not unlike the detective division, is a secondary rather than primary processor of violators of the law.

Arrest statistics make evident the fact that citizens dominate law enforcement through their mobilizations of the

Table 2.9

Percentage Distribution of Arrests of Juveniles (17 years old and under) by Police Division and the Offense Charged in the District of Columbia, 1965

Offense class	Police division						Total percentage	Total number
	Patrol division	Canine division	Morals division	Detective division	Traffic division	Youth-aid division		
Criminal homicide	40	—	—	60	—	—	100	10
Rape and carnal knowledge	29	—	—	66	—	5	100	76
Robbery	83	2	—	14	1	1	101	725
Aggravated assault	91	—	*	1	2	6	100	198
Burglary	94	2	—	3	*	1	100	1,052
Grand larceny	86	—	—	2	2	11	101	63
Unauthorized use of auto	68	3	*	25	2	2	100	725
Arson	86	—	—	10	—	4	100	21
Other felonies	80	1	1	11	1	6	100	164
Total felonies	82	2	*	13	1	2	100	3,034
Total misdemeanors	84	1	*	2	1	12	100	3,230
Grand total	83	2	*	7	1	7	100	6,264

SOURCE: *Annual Report of the Metropolitan Police Department of Washington, D.C., Fiscal Year, 1965*, p. 51.
*Less than 0.5 percent.

patrol division, which, in turn, produces most arrests. Few divisions of a police department devote much attention to proactive work, uncovering crimes and offenders based on their own investigations. The unit of a police department that is most clearly proactive is the vice or morals division. The work of Skolnick shows the essentially proactive strategies and tactics of such units.[16] These observations, for the most part, cannot be applied equally to reactive policing.

It is interesting to note the degree to which the appellate division of our legal system addresses itself to matters that arise primarily from proactive policing of the citizenry, and the degree to which police initiative in moral matters leads to arrest or harassment of citizens. The minimal role of the citizen in bringing such matters to police attention may be based on the fact that the public is often divided over moral matters and such violations often depend on consensual relationships.

Since proactive policing of everyday life is so severely restricted in its capacity to discover and solve most crimes—given the capability of citizens to subvert police work—a substantial change in public attitudes or the law toward morals could substantially reduce proactive policing of everyday life. The Scandinavian countries, most notably Denmark, have shown that such changes can occur in democratic societies.

A proactive strategy of policing everyday life must be pursued when there is a high degree of consensus among citizens who violate the law, while, at the same time public or political pressures demand enforcement of these laws. Crimes against morality, commonly regarded as vice, meet these conditions. Their occurrence is characterized by a high degree of consensus among the participants. And, these are essentially crimes without victims. At the same time, their enforcement depends upon a continuing moral crusade

16. See Skolnick, chaps. 5, 6, and 7.

by other citizens and citizen organizations. Citizens ultimately coerce proactive policing of morals violations by defining themselves and others as victims. Public and political pressures by moral entrepreneurs cast the police in a proactive role in the policing of morals in everyday life precisely because this enforcement depends upon nonparticipants in the violation.

As a parenthetical note, often, even in the policing of events not considered part of everyday life, police employ proactive strategy and tactics when there are no immediate victims of a crime who may act to mobilize them. This applies to matters of subversion and open protest, crimes that threaten the public and political order. Under such extreme conditions, as the proactive policing of subjugated peoples, a citizen's mobilization of the police would leave him open to the accusation and degraded status of collaborationist.

While the policing of motor vehicle traffic is sometimes proactive, it is so for somewhat different reasons. In violations of moving traffic, there are rarely immediate victims to report an offense. Furthermore, our system of enforcing laws for moving traffic generally denies citizens the role of swearing a warrant. In standing vehicle violations, citizens may become very active in mobilizing the police as has been demonstrated by their high participation in calling the police to enforce parking violations in cities like San Francisco. Where parking space is scarce and the public often invades private property to park a vehicle, citizen participation in enforcement is usually high. Nevertheless, the bulk of enforcement for standing vehicle violations occur on public streets and byways, making it primarily a matter for proactive enforcement.

The level of proactive enforcement of moving and standing vehicle violations depends not only upon whether police administrators adopt a proactive strategy with proactive tactics of policing, but also upon whether the department has a specialized unit of enforcement. John Gardiner's study comparing Massachusetts cities with and without specialized traffic units makes this readily apparent.[17] He demonstrates that the enforcement of traffic laws by special traffic divisions leads to higher levels of enforcement for both moving and standing violations of motor vehicle laws. As in the policing of vice, the proactive enforcement of traffic laws may be less a function of the discretion officers have to arrest persons or issue citations than of how the task is organized in the department.

Proactive policing usually alters citizen-police relations. Normally, after a citizen has called to report a crime, police can count on his further support in apprehending the offender. However, in proactive policing such support cannot be readily assumed. Without citizen support in the form of witnesses, the typical proactive policing situation must depend upon officer testimony or other evidence.

When arrests become inputs into other organizations of the criminal-justice system, such as prosecution or the judiciary, their officials often must make judgments about the credibility of the testimony of citizen and police adversaries. Without citizens present, as may often be the case in proactive policing, the case may rest more on evidence than on testimony. But, to make a case on the basis of evidence other than officer or citizen testimony involves considerably more effort for the police than would be required if citizens generated the complaint.

The system of criminal justice adapts in several ways to the dilemmas created by proactive forms of policing. Success in processing police outputs, from arrests made on their own initiative, often depends upon inducing guilty pleas from citizens. And, as far as the citizen is concerned, this may prove a greater threat to him than the exercise of police

17. See John A. Gardiner, "Police Enforcement of Traffic Laws: A Comparative Analysis," in James Q. Wilson, ed., *City Politics and Public Policy* (New York: John Wiley, 1968); and Gardiner, *Traffic and the Police: Variations in Law Enforcement Policy* (Cambridge: Harvard University Press, 1969), chap. 8.

discretion to arrest him. Success also depends upon the extent to which officials in the criminal-justice system accept officer testimony as valid. The general absence of a direct challenge to an officer's testimony by officials of the system stems, in large part, from an investment in maintaining proactive police work.

Discretionary Justice

Conventional views of the criminal-justice system regard citizens primarily in the role of violators of the law and, therefore, as the raw material for the system. The police, on the other hand, are regarded almost exclusively in the role of enforcers of the law, whose decisions, it is believed, create the inputs into the system. We have tried to show here that, in fact, citizens enter the criminal-justice system not only as violators, but more importantly, as enforcers of law. Their discretionary decisions to mobilize the police are a principal source of input into the system, and these decisions profoundly affect the discretion exercised by the police.

The failure to acknowledge the enforcement role of citizens is an important oversight, given the history of justice in the Western World. Historically, the responsibility for law enforcement in criminal matters, and indeed the prosecution of these matters, was largely in the hands of the citizenry.[18] The creation of police bureaucracies in the nineteenth century with enormous power to seek out violations of the law—powers formerly dispersed among inspectorial offices that were not centrally coordinated—appears to have

18. See Seldon D. Bacon, "The Early Development of American Municipal Police: A Study of the Evolution of Formal Controls in a Changing Society" (Ph.D. diss., Yale University, 1939). A definitive statement of the evolution of the office of British police constable is found in Geoffrey Marshall, *Police and Government: The Status and Accountability of the English Constable* (London: Methuen, 1965).

led students of criminal justice to confuse delegated power with the exercise of power. Much of the responsibility for seeking out violations of the law still resides with the citizenry whose responsibility it is to mobilize the police.

Actually, the operating system of criminal justice in the United States is a loosely articulated hierarchy of five major subsystems. The first and lowest of these is the *citizen subsystem,* where vital decisions are made about whether to mobilize the police and cooperate with them, prosecutors, judges, and other officials in the system. The second level is the *law-enforcement or police subsystem* which makes decisions about how to discover crimes, investigate criminal matters, handle noncriminal matters, press for warrants, and book offenders. The *public prosecution subsystem* is third in the hierarchy and decides whether or not a charge is to be pressed, what the charge will be, how evidence is to be secured, and the strategy of prosecution in judicial proceedings. The *misdemeanor and felony courts* must determine substantive and procedural questions of law and of adjudication, where the fate of persons entering guilty pleas, or found guilty, are at stake. The *appellate subsystem* which has the power to grant or deny appeals, is the highest level. There, the fate of the normative order (the law) has priority over decisions about the fate of persons. There is no central ministry of justice to rationally coordinate these member subsystems.

The system of criminal justice is organized as an input-output system. Although each organization in the hierarchy is granted jurisdiction over particular decisions, each also has considerable discretion over what to create or accept as inputs and whether or not to send these inputs on to the next level as outputs. This exercise of discretion critically affects the system of justice, by substantially reducing the amount of output in the movement from one level of the hierarchy to the next. To understand how the criminal-justice system operates, then, we must understand how both delegated and unauthorized discretion[19] affect the quality and quantity of the input and output of cases for each subsystem. For example, there are roles provided for citizen participation at all levels of the system except the appellate. Citizens are expected to call the police for violations of the law, to bear witness before the court, and to serve as jurors. These and other formal roles in each subsystem provide opportunities for exercising unauthorized discretion. Citizens, as noted earlier, by witnessing an action before the police arrive, markedly influence the decisions officers make to arrest or release violators of the law. Delegated as well as unauthorized authority in these different roles allow persons in each subsystem to subvert the goals of other subsystems. Citizens may withhold information from the police or bear false witness in court. The police may do likewise. And the judge may subvert police attempts to control through arrest by wholesale dismissals of certain types of complaints, such as those against prostitution or gambling.

Discretion exercised at any one level of the criminal-justice system may profoundly affect the processing at all other levels, not only because each case moves from one level to another in the hierarchy, but also because each level continues to participate in the processing of that case when it is considered at the next level. The police and the citizen move into the sphere of the prosecutor and all, in turn, into that of the judge. Thus, the police exercise discretion about a case when it is in the police department as well as when it is before the prosecutor and the judge. The problem for each subsystem is how to control the exercise of discretion in any other subsystem, in the interests of both their common and individual goals in the system. The fact that each subsystem derives its legitimacy and authority from

19. See Skolnik, chap. 4, esp. pp. 71–73.

different government jurisdictions and administrators further complicates this matter of control. An understanding of the means one subsystem uses to control the behavior and actions in another is of special interest in comprehending the exercise of discretion.

There is relatively little *formal* provision in the system of criminal justice to control the exercise of discretion by the organizational subordination of some subsystems to others. This lack of organizational subordination makes it difficult for any level to enforce administrative or legal decisions and sanctions over others. The few formal powers any level may have to coerce participation from others— e.g., the court may cite and sanction for contempt of its powers—are easily subverted, even in the short run, by the control each level has over outputs to others.

This kind of structure makes it difficult to resolve conflicts concerning the actual exercise of discretion or the authority to exercise it. We see such conflicts today, between citizens and the police or the police and the appellate division, over police methods of processing citizens. Such conflicts are endemic to the system, since each subsystem is organized more around its central concerns than around those common to the legally constituted system of criminal justice. The police, for example, are more concerned with problems of enforcing the law than they are with those of abstract justice. They are organized to articulate a behavior system of keeping order in public places, responding to citizen complaints about crimes or other matters, and apprehending violators. By contrast, the appellate courts are organized to articulate a moral order—a system of values and norms—rather than a code for behavior in private and public places. The supreme courts are far removed from problems of policing everyday life.

Indeed, the greater the hierarchical distance among the subsystems, the less likely they are to share a common orientation about how to resolve conflicts. Since both the citizens and the police are closer to a behavior system of law and order than are the courts, they often may support one another against the appellate system, despite seemingly conflicting interests.

The legally constituted system of criminal justice has formally provided for the resolution of conflict over substance and procedure by granting priority from the top level of the system on down, with an option to appeal such decisions according to rules. No organizational provision is usually made to see that decisions over normative questions are followed or enforced. The implementation generally rests with the legitimacy of the decision itself. Where compliance is not forthcoming, often the original conflict is translated into questions of moral order. They enter the political sphere as public issues, such as "law and order," to be resolved by political processes, including election to office and legislation.

The absence of organizational provision for controlling discretion makes the subsystems vulnerable to the exercise of unauthorized decisions and sanctions. Paradoxically, the closer subsystems are to one another, the greater their vulnerability to unauthorized discretion by the other. This is most apparent in citizen and police subsystems. Popular opinion emphasizes the vulnerability of citizens to police discretion, particularly in the use of force. The police, however, are highly vulnerable to citizen discretion, not only through the citizens' immediate power to mobilize and cooperate with them, but also through their political power in communities. The political control of the citizenry over the police takes many forms. On the one hand, citizens can exercise considerable influence over the appointment of officers—as they have most recently with regard to race—while, on the other hand, the "protection" political parties and officials afford organized or syndicated crime is well documented. Indeed, the subversive capacity of the citizenry on the police undoubtedly is far greater than their subversive capacity for the bench.

In the relative absence of some formal organizational provision for control over discretion in the subsystems, the major form of control one subsystem has over others, is exercised *within* each subsystem. This is based on what the various subsystems share in common, viz., the processing of the *same* people and information. The major means they have to control others are discretionary decisions regarding these same people and information. But they can do so only when these decisions enter their own subsystem. In this way, the prosecutor controls the police with regard to the criminal charge; he may refuse to accept the police charge as bona fide. Similarly, judges deny cases or information about them if *their* rules are not followed. Citizens of course can control information to any level, beginning with their capacity to mobilize the police.

Counterstrategies necessarily emerge to limit the control exercised by another subsystem. A major technique is to withhold information or output. Withholding information is particularly effective when there are restrictions on organizational capacity to develop information. The police can effectively control prosecutors in this way, since most prosecutors have little organizational capacity to develop information. Withholding output obviates the necessity to play according to the others' rules. For example, the police need only conform to the rules of prosecutors and judges on matters it sends to them, but not in those matters it handles by internal means such as harassment by refusal to arrest or book, or failure to request prosecution, thereby dropping charges.

Another common technique is to overload the next level. The police may do this by mass arrest, as often happens when there are issues over the policing of deviants. Overload of the system by mass arrest may be particularly troublesome to the prosecutor and the courts, as recent experience with urban riots and student dissent eloquently testify.[20]

The fact that the major means of control among the subsystems is *internal* to each subsystem has important consequences. The first is that *procedural rather than substantive issues dominate the system of criminal justice.* The "test" applied is: Was legal procedure followed? In other words, were the arrest, search of the person or his property, the confession, made through lawful means? Another consequence is that *each subsystem creates its own system of justice,* thereby subverting the ends of the larger system of justice. Much of the justice by citizens, police, and prosecutor is justice without a court trial. Each subsystem, moreover, seeks to protect itself from penetration by the other through *erecting informal as well as formal barriers to contact and communication.* The back-room and hallway-plea bargaining of the prosecutor are no more easily penetrated than are the lock-up and blue curtain of the police. Finally, *cooptation becomes a major means of controlling other subsystems;* the practice of police and prosecutors bargaining with defense counsel over the defendant's plea is the most common example.

20. See note: "The Administration of Justice in the Wake of the Detroit Civil Disorder of July, 1967," *Michigan Law Review* 66 (May 1968): 1542–1630, and note: "Criminal Justice in Extremis: Administration of Justice During the April, 1968 Chicago Disorder," *The University of Chicago Law Review* 361 (Spring 1969): 455–613.

III

POLICE MANNERS AND MORALS

Standards for conduct arise whenever it is assumed that people may exercise discretion over behavior. Where matters of discretion over the conduct of others is central, law is crucial, just as ethics is pivotal in matters of discretion concerning deportment. To examine how the organization of police discretion over citizens affects police standards of conduct and the behavior of citizens and police toward one another, we will deal with policing as an occupation that shares important elements with other occupations called professions.

Police work in the United States is an occupation identified with a particular kind of work organization, most commonly a municipal police department, a county sheriff's office, or the State police. Traditionally, all of the jobs in such police organizations have been held by persons "sworn to duty" and allegiance to the department. This identification of police work with common membership in a work organization generates an occupational culture of policing that affects police standards of law enforcement and justice as well as their conduct at work.

Police Work as a Profession

A profession is commonly regarded as a special kind of occupation where technical knowledge is gained through long, prescribed training. The knowledge itself is regarded as a systematic body of theory and practice. The professional person adheres to a set of professional norms that stipulate the practitioner should do technically competent work in the "client's" interest. As Wilensky notes, at the core of professionalism is devotion to an ideal that " . . . the client's interest more than personal or commercial profit should guide decisions when the two are in conflict."[1]

This description characterizes all of the established or "free" professions, but it omits one essential quality. The core of any profession is a *practice* with persons or organizations as clients. And, the professional, in his practice, must make a *decision* in which he has *discretion* to decide something about the client's future. Such decisions may be called diagnoses, determinations, evaluations, judgments, even findings. Yet basically they are decisions about the *fate* of the client.

Some professional decisions about a person's future are given as *advice,* which the person may follow or ignore. Other professional decisions about a person's fate are made to organizational clients and that person may have no choice in the decisions. When a person is unable to exercise discretion about the professional determination, we speak of *coerced* decisions. The teacher, for example, decides whether pupils shall pass or fail just as the judge decides what constitutes a bona fide case and the disposition that shall be made of it. To be sure, where decisions about the fate of people are made within organizations, there may be options to appeal them. Yet such appeals also eventuate in a decision about a person's fate.

There are many occupations in America that claim status as professions, however, many of these—such as engineering, advertising and even undertaking—lack the core element I use to define a "profession." These occupations do

1. Harold Wilensky, "The Professionalization of Everyone?" *The American Journal of Sociology* 70 (September 1964): 138–40.

not require making decisions that involve technical and moral judgments affecting the fate of people.[2] The police in America belong to one of the few occupations that includes all of the essential elements to qualify as a profession. They possess the power of coercive authority, and through their power to arrest and book for offenses, they control the fate of "clients." Furthermore, the code of ethics for law-enforcement officers is the same as for any profession. Law-enforcement officers are sworn to duty at all times and must discharge this duty with honor to themselves and others.

Duty perhaps means more to the police than it does to those who work in occupations that lay more legitimate claims to the status of professions. Policing is one of the few "moral call" occupations. Police are duty bound to come when and where called, regardless of who calls them. Like clergymen, they serve others in matters of moral crisis and dilemma. But, as in the military, they must be prepared to follow orders and give their lives in the line of duty.

Although professional decisions presume latitude in choice and responsibility for making these choices, there are, invariably, boundaries limiting that discretion and responsibility. These boundaries may be determined by the culture of the profession and any subcultures within it, legal requirements controlling the profession, and client or system requirements that limit access to professionals and their practice. Moreover, whenever professionals work within organizations, the organization sets additional limits on the exercise of discretion. The constraints on discretion that arise in a paramilitary bureaucracy such as a police department necessarily pose dilemmas and contradictions for the professional status and practice of the police.

A *bureaucracy* requires the standardization of rules by a central authority in the expectation that universalism will

2. There is another class of occupations and roles where decisions are made about the fate of organizations: Administration. Administrators, of course, may make judgments that qualify as professional.

prevail in the application of these rules. This contradicts the concept that in a profession, the professional must be able to exercise discretion in the application of standards, particularly to meet the requirements of a particular case. A *command organization* threatens professional status because it expects men to follow orders regardless of their judgment. The professional ideal holds that orders are antithetical to the exercise of discretion.

All bureaucracies, then, pose problems for the exercise of professional discretion. These problems are exacerbated for the police, who, in a command bureaucracy, are expected to obey the rules and follow the orders of superiors and, at the same time, to exercise their professional discretion. In other words, a typical line policeman is expected both to adhere to commands and be held responsible for all discretion exercised in the line of duty. To understand the standards of police work and how the police exercise discretion, it is necessary to examine how the bureaucratically organized police department with a cen-. tralized command and control affects officers.

Bureaucratic Organization of Police Work

The core of modern police departments is the centralized communications center where decisions are made to activate men. The line officer on patrol is commanded from a central headquarters, and this sharply limits his use of discretion concerning what constitutes police work. Moreover, the centralization of command and control in police department also restricts the discretion local precinct commanders and supervisors may exercise over the line officer. Although the line officer has little authority to exercise discretion about what he will investigate when he is commanded, he must exercise considerable discretion about how to conduct that investigation, whether it should be an official matter, and whether he should make a decision that will affect the

fate of citizens. His autonomy in these matters results from
the control he has over the *acquisition* of information for
decisions. Of course, when he operates in preventive patrol
and is permitted to pursue matters on his own, his discretion
is even greater. No doubt, part of the resistance of line
police officers to mobile patrol commanded by central radio
dispatch stems from resistance to limitations on their discretion. Until the advent of the two-way radio, it was difficult to command the line officer, because the police patrol,
unlike the military, operates as a dispersed command of
individuals or very small groups without supervision.

The bureaucratization of police organizations threatens
the autonomy of line officers in several other ways. It limits
their exclusive jurisdiction over decisions by fragmenting
the decision-making process and distributing it among various groups in different roles, each of which makes claims to
professional competence in decisions about the same case. It
may also restrict professional autonomy by instituting procedures for the review of decisions. The detective division
of many police departments, for example, restricts the
autonomy of line officers in both of these ways by giving the
detective jurisdiction over all subsequent investigation as
well as authority to review line officers' decisions.

Specialization within the police bureaucracy may limit
professional autonomy in another way. It does not so much
limit the exercise of discretion, as it limits the ideal that the
professional serve the client. For example, the development
of a special "human-relations" staff, will remove an important function from the domain of the line worker, thus restricting the professionalization of his work. Without specific
provision for implementation in the line, there is little opportunity to apply human-relations to the treatment of clients.

Disputes over Jurisdiction

The granting of exclusive jurisdiction to the professional

person in making a decision about a client is often infringed upon by the bureaucratization of decision making.[3] This is especially true when more than one group of professionals is given jurisdiction over the same case.

The decisions of criminal and appellate courts, defining the limits of interrogation, search of the person and property, the seizure of evidence, and the use of force, have been characterized by the police and the courts as restrictions on discretion. The legal view is that the police have exercised too much discretion in their relationships with the public and that decisions as to method are to be made on legal rather than on police professional grounds. A prevailing view is that the police must be controlled by more legitimate authority, authority that is vested in the law, the public prosecutor, the courts, and in external civil review procedures.

The dilemma faced by the police in legal review is a classic case of dispute over competence and jurisdiction. A group of professionals—in this case made up largely of lawyers and jurists—seeks to restrict the powers of would-be-professionals, the police. This conflict resembles those between medical doctors and nurses or prosecutors and judges. Jurisdictional conflicts are endemic where one group of professionals controls the fate of the decisions made by another group of professionals (or aspirants to professional status) in an intricately balanced system of organization.

Much of the conflict between the courts and the police is in a sense inevitable, given our system of law enforcement and criminal justice. The system institutionalizes the introduction of clients into the police organization by delegating to the police the power of arrest and control over information related to it, while the power of assessing the outcome of the arrest and determining police procedure on evidence is institutionalized in the prosecutor and the courts. In reaction to this denial of their claims to professional competence

3. See Wilensky, p. 148.

and their ability to exercise discretion in making decisions, the police develop a subculture with practices that justify their claim to exclusive jurisdiction over "police matters."

Conflicts over professional competence and jurisdiction also tend to arise in professional training where the experienced professional regards the trainee with distrust and severely restricts his opportunity to make discretionary decisions, whereby he would be able to gain the experience requisite to professional competence. Howard Becker has pointed out that this conflict is an essential ingredient in the production of student cultures in professional schools.[4] The failure of most police cadet programs within police departments results from such a bureaucratic restriction on the exercise of discretion by "trained" persons ineligible by age for sworn police duty.

Civilian review boards are an organizational mechanism designed to penetrate the exclusive jurisdiction of police departments over their decisions and service to clients. Apart from questions of how external review affects administrative authority, any such procedure makes problematic the professional control of professional practice. What a civilian review board does, in effect, is monitor practice by setting itself up to review client complaints about practice. However, the monitoring of professional practice is zealously guarded by professional groups. Though no professional group is entirely free from an external monitor—inasmuch as there are at least some conditions for judicial proceedings charging malpractice—the traditional professions have tried to retain virtually complete control of standards of practice, arguing essentially that members of a profession are the most qualified to judge the competence of other members. Even where professionals are employees of public organizations, such as public hospitals, civil service review has generally operated to review complaints by the organization against the em-

4. Howard S. Becker et al., *Boys in White: Student Culture in Medical School* (Chicago: University of Chicago Press, 1961).

ployee (or vice versa) and only rarely complaints by clients against the professional or the organization. Any external review board imposes a barrier to professional control by attenuating the latitude an occupation or an organization based on an occupation has to police itself.

Professional Control by Associations of Professionals

Historically, police organizations have failed to develop universal standards for control of practice by members of the police occupation. Most police organizations are local associations, such as the Patrolmen's Benevolent Association, with no more than nominal membership in a larger association of policemen and certainly without claim to exclusive control over the police profession. The dilemma confronting both police officers and their administrators is that with control of police practice lodged in a local, bureaucratically organized police department, with occasional civil service or legal review, they are unable to convince the public that police service is trustworthy.

Faced with either administrative or external review of police practice and lacking the protection of collegial forms of review, police officers increasingly opt for union rather than professional ways to handle complaints about police practice or about their employer infringing on their rights and obligations. Controversies over professional matters are settled either through collective bargaining between police union and management or by the courts before which the unions have brought these matters. In this way, questions of the professional competence of officers are translated into questions of employee rights subject to collective bargaining and arbitration. Union contracts with provisions for seniority, promotion from within the ranks, and evaluation procedures are substituted for professional evaluation. Written civil-service examinations rather than professional judgment become the standard for evaluating competence. Questions of misconduct in the performance of duty are readily translated into constitutional rights of police officers under investigation for misconduct. The 1970 review of corruption in the New York City Police Department by a special commission of the city government was confronted with a suit brought jointly by the New York Civil Liberties Union and the Police Sergeants Benevolent Association blocking the questioning of sergeants by the commission. The line officer's PBA sought further to enjoin the commission from any investigation on the grounds that a city charter provision outlawed any review board that had a majority of members who were not in the New York Police Department.[5]

It is unclear just what the consequences are, for both the professionals and their clients, of having a union as opposed to a professional model. What is clear is that the collective-bargaining model poses constraints on professional review. The police, in enforcing the law and catching criminals, must balance traditional moral and quasi-legal concerns with other contemporary concerns, such as the legality of police methods and civil rights. "Professionalization" of police work is a legitimate way to deal with this dilemma provided one can convince the public that police service is trustworthy.

Standards of Discretionary Enforcement

The line police officer, like all professionals, must make a decision that determines the fate of the client. Only some of his decisions will be evaluated by others both inside and outside the department. Certain of these decisions influence not only the fate of the client but also that of the public. Often, too, the decision involves the fate of a social relation-

5. See David Burnham, "Two Inspectors Demoted in Inquiry on Corruption," *New York Times,* November 17, 1970, p. 1; and David Burnham, "City Graft Inquiry Seeks U.S. Funds," *New York Times,* November 25, 1970, p. 1.

ship, a family unit, an organization, or the state of public order.

Many other decisions frequently must be made before a police officer can arrive at a decision of "fate." Some of these are of a technical nature: should the matter be regarded as civil or criminal; should the officer detain or arrest a citizen. But, others pertain to the kind of information necessary to arrive at a final decision: what other units might be mobilized to provide that information; what is needed for testimony, and so on. Unlike the lawyer or judge, who may take a long time gathering information to make a diagnosis or reviewing the decisions that lead up to a fate decision, a line officer often must make a quick fate decision. This creates, in many ways, a paradoxical situation for the police. To be professional about the decision often means that more information and more time is required. However, to protect the interests of the client and the public, and to satisfy requirements of operating efficiency, a quick decision is required. The resolution of such a dilemma in the long run may require changes in both the law and police organization, substantially altering the concept of arrest.

Police decisions are further complicated by an officer's own sense of justice. To be sure, while more "professional" advice is available to the patrolman from his superiors, most decisions must be his. They must be not only correct but, putting aside legal pretenses, both the police and the public sense that they must also be just.

To complicate matters further, some decisions by the officer, as indicated previously, will be evaluated by others both within and outside the department. These superiors will regard it as their prerogative to solicit information from the officer and, most certainly, to withhold a decision for indefinite periods of time while they exercise their "professional" judgment. Inevitably, then, an officer who makes a decision that will be processed within and outside the department makes a decision that later is subject to review.

The patrol officer occupies a crucial position in the system of criminal justice because he controls the original input of information upon which all subsequent processing of a case depends. However, subsequent decision-makers may review this information. This creates a conflict between the line officer and all those who later process the case, since each level of the hierarchy seeks control of the decision. Those who will process the case within the police department—e.g., the detectives—claim they are more "professional," thereby relegating the patrol officer to the role of a technician. Those who are outside the organization—e.g., public prosecutors and judges—seek a decision on technical grounds, considering professional decisions as falling within the province of the law and, thus, to be made by lawyers.

Whenever people in a number of roles in different organizations have the power to make decisions about the same case, problems of overlapping jurisdiction with competing rights to make the decision arise. And, where professionals are involved, there are competing claims of professional competence to make the decision. The role of the patrol officer, at the lowest rank in the hierarchy of decision making, is most vulnerable to counterclaims of competence and is the least defensible. Paradoxically, it is the line officer's original decision that controls whether law-enforcement and criminal-justice agents can process the decision at all. Thus, although he has the greatest range of opportunity to exercise discretion, and therefore of possibilities to exercise professional judgment, he also is the most susceptible in the system of law enforcement and criminal justice to limitations on the use of his discretion.

The ground rules for determining final decisions within the broad interpretative powers granted within and under the criminal law will undoubtedly continue to be set in our legal system by lawyers through the courts. Their position as the "more professional" means that they will resist claims by the police to provide more definite ground rules.

Indeed, the public prosecutor, for example, will insist upon his right of "choice" among the charges that the police bring against an individual, and the courts will insist upon their review of these choices and all evidence pertaining thereto. Yet the police will continue to insist upon broader jurisdiction and greater discretion. What is especially important is that, since the police occupy the crucial position for any case entering the legal system, they are most capable of subverting the system of justice. When the police are denied professional autonomy in decisions, they employ their capacity to subvert by applying justice on their own terms. What is more, this opens the way for officers to individually and collectively define justice.

Paradoxically, in our legal system, matters that the police want defined by rules, the courts want to leave open to discretion. And what the courts want defined by rules, the police want to leave open to discretion. Thus the courts want police procedures to be clear, definite, and unambiguously defined, but they want matters of substance to be left open to argument and decision, and even to new interpretation and precedent. For them, precedent governs but does not rule. The police, on the other hand, want to be left with broad discretion in enforcing the law, obtaining information, and determining procedures for handling clients, but they want the courts to make clear how substance is to be applied and what is a bona fide case.

Whenever participants in a number of roles in different organizations have authority to make decisions about the fate of the same clients, and the authority to make these decisions is hierarchically determined so that the decision at each level is open to review at the next, the stage is set for conflict among the participants. Conflict is most likely to occur when, as in our system of criminal justice, there is little opportunity for common review and each level defines its decisions as the most competent and moral. Ambiguous definitions of organizational goals and jurisdiction and the failure to recognize or acknowledge differences in claims to competence, will continue to provoke conflict among the participants and the police will still be regarded as nonprofessional. The courts will continue to be wrapped in the cloak of "justice" and the police will parade the banners of "crime-stoppers," "crook-catchers," and "law and order." The system will not rise to the problem of common professional concern.

The criminal-justice system is primarily an information-processing system. Much of the conflict among participants and organizations in the system arises over the control of the quantity and quality of information. Interrogation, search and seizure of evidence, and detention for purposes of acquiring information, become normative issues precisely because each subsystem has different standards as to how information is to be acquired and used. Moreover, it can enforce those standards by controlling information output to the level above it in the hierarchy and by refusing to receive information from the level below. The citizen controls the police by withholding information; the prosecution and the courts refuse information acquired by the police. Failure to comply with standards for information even leads to the refusal to process the people about whom one has information. An example of this is when the prosecutor refuses to prefer charges because the police infringed upon the rights of the accused.

Much of the conflict between the police and the prosecutor or the courts depend, then, upon differences in standards for acquiring, evaluating and using information. Therefore, the police must not only be concerned about the use they make of information but also about how this use is evaluated at other levels in the hierarchy. Much of the information processed depends upon an officer's oral testimony. The prosecutor, defense lawyers, or the judge may question a police officer to elicit information in a conventional sense. However, when they later evaluate the means whereby this information was acquired, they may treat the police as adversaries, provoking further conflict.

Police officers occupy a unique role in the system of criminal justice. In their relations with citizens, whereby inputs are introduced into the system, they occupy the role of interrogator, and command authority; but when they generate outputs, they are themselves subject to interrogation, submitting to another's authority. These reversals in role and status generate conflicts for officers, particularly when their testimonies, methods of acquiring information, and exercise of discretion are challenged at other levels of the system. Analogous problems arise for prosecutors and judges under review, a matter not considered here.

Police Justice

Another major source of conflict between the police and other legal officers is the way police exercise discretion in making an arrest. Consider how a police officer typically handles a situation that may lead to an arrest. The officer invariably makes a judgment that some criminal statute has been violated, thereby satisfying the legal criterion of arrest on probable cause. But police officers in America do more than that, since there is a high probability an officer will not make an arrest when he satisfies probable cause. Our observations of citizen initiated encounters with the police, for example, show that officers decided not to make arrests of one or more suspects for 43 percent of all felonies and 52 percent of all misdemeanors judged by observers as situations where an arrest could have been made on probable cause.[6] Something other than probable cause is required, then, for the officer to make an arrest.

For the police, that something else is a *moral belief* that the law should be enforced and the violation sanctioned by

6. See Donald J. Black, "Police Encounters and Social Organization" (Ph.D. diss., University of Michigan, 1968), table 33.

the criminal-justice system. The line officer usually reaches that decision by conducting an investigation to establish probable cause and by conducting a "trial" to determine who is guilty. His decision, therefore, is in an important sense judicial. This judicial determination will be influenced, as it is in the courts, by the deference and demeanor of the suspect, argument as to mitigating circumstances, complainant preferences for justice, and the willingness of the complainant to participate in seeing that it is done. All in all, an officer not only satisfies probable cause but also concludes after his careful evaluation that *the suspect is guilty and an arrest is therefore just*.

Observation of the transactions between police and citizens validate the officer's determination of guilt. Without exception, the observer concluded that the suspect in the 255 arrests observed in these encounters had in fact violated the law. Observers and officers occasionally did not agree about the specific offense(s) to be charged, but there was no disagreement as to the suspect's guilt in violating some criminal statute.

Furthermore, our observations of transactions between line police and citizens that lead to an arrest convince us that the arrest and determination of guilt is, on the average, based on more information than generally will be available or processed at any other level of the criminal-justice system. There are exceptions, of course. Ordinarily, however, such factors as the memory of witnesses and officers, the number of witnesses, and the restructuring of information to conform to legal criteria, alters subsequent processing of information. From the perspective of those in legal roles, these changes in the quantity and quality of information are viewed as inevitable or necessary, and therefore of no major consequence for the system of justice. Hardly so for the officer.

The experiences in the encounter create dilemmas for officers and set the stage for their conflict with other officials in the system of criminal justice. Given their investment in making a decision to arrest and a firm conviction that it is just, they believe that justice should be done by others as well. This belief in justice, of course, has been tempered by experience in the system and the full awareness that there is "bargain justice" played according to the lawyers' rules. Indeed the police often stereotype other participants in the system. Citizens "cop out"; defense lawyers have "clout"; the prosecutor "deals under the table"; judge X "throws the book." Indeed when an officer wants justice done, he may tailor his case accordingly. He may seek out a particular prosecutor or book for a particular court (if he has that option).

Sometimes an officer makes more than an ordinary investment in a case, and he becomes indignant when justice is not done. Several conditions give rise to high investment in seeing justice done. Moral indignation is one, particularly if it stems from the failure of an offender to grant deference to police authority. The officer, then, wants justice done to punish disrespectful demeanor toward *his* authority. Observation of police and citizen transactions show that an officer is more likely to arrest a juvenile or an adult offender when deference is withheld than when it is granted. Whether or not a complainant is present in citizen initiated encounters, the citizens who behave antagonistically toward the officer are more likely to be arrested than those who are civil or very deferential. Black reports that when complainants are present, 72 percent of the adults who behave antagonistically toward the police are arrested in the field while only 45 percent of those who are civil and 40 percent of those who are deferential toward the police are arrested.[7] There is similar evidence that police arrest in response to antagonism from juveniles.[8]

7. Ibid., pp. 216–23, 229–32, 252–58.
8. Donald J. Black and Albert J. Reiss, Jr., "Police Control of Juveniles," *American Sociological Review* 35 (February 1970): 63–77.

The organization of the input-output system also frustrates an officer's own sense of justice. Whenever another level of the system fails to affirm an officer's arrest decision, the client is returned to the community and is again that officer's responsibility. Repeated offenders who, from the officer's perspective, are dealt with leniently by other levels of the system, fall into this category. Officers are, for this reason, particularly opposed to the repeated release of juveniles on probation.

Patrol officers commonly regard juveniles as the most difficult class of citizens to police and the most leniently handled in the system of justice. Our survey interviews with officers in high-crime-rate precincts of Boston, Chicago, and Washington, D.C., disclose that 80 percent of all officers thought juveniles were harder to deal with now than formerly. This is almost double the percentage for dealing with "people in his precinct." The main ways in which officers perceived it to be harder to cope with juveniles were that they show less respect for law and authority (20 percent), they are more aggressive, defiant, and rebellious (24 percent), and they are more aware of restrictions on police conduct (22 percent).[9] A considerable number of officers who policed in these areas also expressed negative judgments about the operating legal system; 54 percent of all officers, for example, regarded juvenile court judges as too lenient and only 16 percent thought the judges behaved in a fair or just manner. Similarly, 59 percent of all officers regarded municipal court judges as too lenient and only 26 percent saw them as on the whole fair or just.[10] At times, officers in a police department may regard the juvenile court judges so negatively that an open attack on the court develops. During

9. See Albert J. Reiss, Jr., "Career Orientations, Job Satisfaction, and the Assessment of Law Enforcement Problems by Police Officers," in President's Commission on Law Enforcement and the Administration of Justice, *Studies in Crime and Law Enforcement in Major Metropolitan Areas,* Field Surveys III, vol. 2, sec. 2 (Washington, D.C.: USGPO, 1967), table 40.
10. Ibid., table 47.

the spring of 1969, such an attack was waged by the police officers in Ypsilanti, Michigan, against the Washtenaw County Juvenile Court. The major complaint of the officers was that they could not control juveniles when the court continued to release them without formal sanctions.[11] Regardless of their merit, such charges bring into the open the cleavage between the police and judges over issues of justice and the sanctioning of offenders.

The judgments of the police and of others in the legal system are intricately balanced in a commitment to justice. If, on the average, the officer's sense of justice is not confirmed, or if his moral commitments are not sustained by others, he loses his own moral commitment to the system. Where moral commitment is lost, subcultural practices take over. One such practice that exacerbates the relationship of the police with the public is harassment.

Police Harassment

Police resort to harassment under conditions where they are caught between their own, or others', expectations that they control unlawful conduct, while other levels of the system thwart such enforcement by failing to treat their arrests of citizens seriously. Actually, one can predict that harassment will become police policy or unofficial practice whenever citizen influence compels the police to make arrests that are systematically disregarded by others in the criminal-justice system. The harassment of juveniles, minorities, and even of those engaged in vice can be predicted, based on these factors.

It is altogether predictable that the police will harass citizens. In fact, it is a general strategy that citizens frequently use under similar conditions. For example, some citizens of Kew Gardens, Queens, New York, when disgruntled with

11. *Ann Arbor News,* April 11, 1969.

what they regarded as failure to police homosexuals in a
local park (a failure they attributed more to city control of
the police than to the police as such) formed a vigilante committee to harass the homosexuals by "policing" the area with
powerful flashlights and walkie-talkies. A Mr. Tashman reported to the *New York Times* that "when the homosexuals
appeared, the men would surround them, shine the lights in
their faces, and tell them to get out." As a final move, they
cut down all shrubs and trees.[12] Similarly, college students
and civil rights workers found that harassment is an effective
means of extralegal control, taking such forms as the sit-in,
the mill-in, or disruption of ordered events by some other
tactic.

The processing of cases in the system of criminal justice
also frustrates officers and further encourages the creation
of an officer culture of justice. Citizens and police, those who
initiate inputs, characteristically assess the behavior of persons, while prosecutors and judges characteristically assess
information to insure that justice is done. Paradoxically,
those farthest removed from observing criminal behavior—
the criminal court judges—make the final judgment about
the behavior.

Often an officer views the judge's decision as justice subverted, because for him a case is not isolated. Rather it is a
part of an order of behavior and events that he, the officer,
is expected to control in a specified way. These seemingly
different approaches in dealing with such matters encourage
police subcultures to do their own justice, an extreme instance of which is illustrated by reports of police behavior in
Brazil. There, it is reported, that the police have taken to
murdering leaders in organized crime out of a conviction that
the system of justice is unjust.[13] A problem with any system
of criminal justice, where the final decision rests outside the

12. *New York Times,* July 1, 1969, pp. 1, 29; also July 2, 1969, p. 68.
13. *Time Magazine,* April 25, 1969, p. 61.

control of those who previously decided the matter, is to prevent their alienation.

Our system of criminal justice tends to alienate the police by accentuating status and prestige inequalities among officials in the system. By failing to show deference and by a condescending demeanor, lawyers, prosecutors, and judges often demean the status of the officer, by treating him as less professional. Furthermore, many officers become particularly sensitive when the bench fails to treat seriously a lack of deference to police authority while demanding total deference to judicial authority. Citizen behavior that the officer must tolerate, the judge will not. Many judges who regard contempt of police authority as part of the officer's job are quick to sanction defendants for far less serious infractions in court. Even more infuriating to the officer is how citizens change their behavior for the court from what it was when they made the arrest. The officer relives his experience with offenders and sees them as they were; the prosecutor or judge cannot.

Police subculture consists, then, in part, of developing standards of doing justice. Justice becomes necessary in the eyes of the police when deference is violated, when outcomes violate their sense of justice, when they are degraded in status, and when their efforts to control are subverted by other organizations in the subsystem. Of course, there are other factors which promote the development of a subculture, particularly attempts to sanction the police through punishment. We shall explore some of these later.

Exemplary Police Conduct

The conduct of the police at work and as representatives of a moral order is as much at issue in our society as are the police standards for performing their official duties to arrest on probable cause and maintain order. The police, in short, are expected to fulfill the expectations of a "moral call" profession; they are expected to lead exemplary lives.

We shall deal only with their exemplary conduct while on duty, since little is known about their moral conduct when they are not on duty. The police are expected to violate no laws of moral or legal conduct while on duty. They also are expected to behave according to the department's code of "conduct becoming an officer" and to follow all rules and regulations. In considering an officer's conduct in upholding the law, it is clear that he often fails to arrest citizens for violations of the law. As previously noted, that lies within his sphere of discretion, since at law and by official policy he is permitted to exercise discretion in making an arrest. To be sure, he can be cited by the department for failure to exercise discretion properly or for lax enforcement, but the boundaries in these matters are far from clear.

An examination of the officer's conduct on duty must, therefore, be limited to considering his unlawful behavior and his failure to obey the department's rules and regulations. Unlawful conduct is of two kinds. The officer may use unlawful means in enforcing the law or he may engage in unlawful conduct by violating the laws that apply to all citizens. Infractions of department rules vary considerably in their seriousness. The more serious infractions are neglect of duty, drinking while on duty, and falsification of information, since these clearly affect the quality and performance of duty.

Unwarranted Use of Police Authority

The unwarranted use of authority toward citizens includes a variety of charges relative to the employment of illegal means such as the undue use of force and threats, harassment, uncivil treatment through abusive language and demeaning epithets, and the application of illegal means in investigation, e.g., illegal search and seizure of evidence.

Precise estimates of the extent to which the police engage in unwarranted conduct toward citizens are lacking. Available data come from three different methods of data collection: sample surveys of a cross-section of citizens, formal complaints to police authorities and boards or to civil review agencies, and observations of police and citizen transactions. A number of conclusions about the nature, extent, and causes of police misconduct toward citizens may be drawn from these studies.

The use of illegal means of investigation and of incivility toward citizens seems far more common than the misuse of force and threats in police contacts with citizens. Questioning of a sample of citizens in fifteen cities about police misconduct for the National Advisory Commission on Civil Disorders showed 22 percent of all Negroes and 6 percent of all whites reported they had been frisked or searched without good reason, and 20 percent of all Negroes and 9 percent of all whites said the police had been disrespectful or used insulting language. Smaller proportions, 7 percent of all Negroes and 2 percent of all whites, said they had been roughed up by the police at some time.[14]

Evidence of a similar sort (table 3.1) is available from our observation of 13,939 citizens in 5,012 police and citizen transactions. Police officers openly ridiculed or belittled 5 percent of all citizens, and they were observed behaving in a brusque or authoritarian manner toward another 5 percent. Three percent of all citizens claimed the police behaved with threatening, hostile, or provocative conduct. Observers judged the use of force to be excessive for only about 3 in 1000 citizens in these encounters.

The rates from surveys based on citizen experiences are consistent with these data obtained from our own observations in showing that undue use of force is far less frequent than other forms of police misconduct toward citizens. Incivility toward citizens and illegal practices in law enforce-

14. Angus Campbell and Howard Schuman, "Racial Attitudes in Fifteen American Cities," *Supplemental Studies for the National Advisory Commission on Civil Disorders* (Washington, D.C.: USGPO, 1969), table IV.

Table 3.1
Percentage Distributions of the Demeanor of Citizens and Conduct of Police Officers in 13,939 Citizen and Police Transactions

Demeanor of citizen toward officer	Conduct of police officer toward citizen					Total percentage
	Personal (2,133)*	Civil (10,092)	Demeaning (645)	Authoritarian (655)	Threatening, hostile, provocative (414)	
Percentage by demeanor of citizen in response to conduct of officer						
Very deferential (1,647)*	26	64	4	3	3	100
Civil (11,143)	15	76	3	4	2	100
Antagonistic (1,149)	6	52	16	16	10	100
Total	15	72	5	5	3	100
Percentage by conduct of office in response to citizen demeanor						
Very deferential (1,647)	20	10	10	7	12	12
Civil (11,143)	77	84	61	65	61	80
Antagonistic (1,149)	3	6	29	28	27	8
Total	100	100	100	100	100	100

SOURCE: *Studies of Crime and Law Enforcement in Major Metropolitan Areas*, table 5.

*Figures in parentheses indicate number of transactions.

ment seem far common. The high rates based on experiences seem reasonable if one simply assumes that over time police misconduct is directed toward different citizens.

Reciprocity in Civility

Transactions between citizens and the police are usually civil. Both citizens and the police behaved civilly in 83 percent of the transactions we observed. When citizens behave other than civilly toward officers, they are somewhat more likely to behave with deference than with antagonism. Eighty percent of all citizens were civil toward the police, 12 percent were very deferential, and 8 percent antagonistic (See table 3.1). However, when officers do not treat citizens civilly, they are as likely to respond with demeaning, authoritarian, hostile, threatening, and provocative forms of behavior as they are to treat citizens with respect as persons. Based on our observations, the behavior of officers was civil toward 72 percent, personal toward 15 percent, and uncivil toward 13 percent of all citizens (see table 3.1).

An inescapable conclusion is that officers are somewhat more likely to be uncivil toward citizens than citizens are toward officers. While in 83 percent of all transactions both officers and citizens behaved civilly to one another, in 13 percent of these transactions, only one party behaved civilly. The citizen was the civil party in 8 percent of these encounters and the officer in 5 percent.

There is a striking lack of reciprocity in incivility. While officers or citizens displayed antagonism in 17 percent of all encounters, it was reciprocated in only 4 percent. Whenever incivility occurs in an encounter, the chances are only 1 in 6 that the other party will reciprocate with incivility. This lack of reciprocity in incivility is the central problem in explaining uncivil conduct by either citizens or the police.

Uncivil behavior on the part of police officers may be

partially explained by examining institutions and their organization in the encounter. The role of the citizen in the encounter and exercise of police authority are related to the legitimacy of police authority.

The citizen's role in the encounter clearly sets conditions for officer behavior. Generally those who mobilize the police —the complainants—support the police in the encounter, while citizens who are regarded as suspects or offenders by either the complainant or the police are adversaries. Other people present, such as witnesses or informants, are also likely to support police goals in the encounter. Bystanders, however, may show support or hostility, depending upon conditions leading to the mobilization of the police and the nature of the encounter. When the police enter a situation on their own initiative, bystanders are more likely to question the legitimacy of their intervention and, therefore, respond with hostility. This is especially true when they intervene in public settings where consensual support for police intervention is low.

Our observations of police and citizen encounters show quite clearly that most citizens, regardless of their roles, are civil toward the police. Almost three-fourths of offenders or suspects and about 85 percent of complainants and citizens in other roles were civil toward the police. Similarly, roles play a very small part in the proportions of citizens showing high deference toward the police in the encounter. Nevertheless, offenders were five times more likely than complainants to establish an antagonistic relationship with the police. Actually, 71 percent of all antagonistic behavior toward the police was exhibited by suspects (see table 3.2). It is apparent that the adversary role of suspect is the one most closely associated with antagonistic behavior toward the police.

Although the police usually respond civilly or deal with citizens in a personal manner, regardless of their role, a disproportionate amount of uncivil behavior on the part of

Table 3.2

Percentage Distributions for Conduct of Citizen by Role of Citizen in
13,939 Encounters with the Police

Role of citizen	Conduct of citizen			Total per-centage
	Very deferential (1,647)*	Civil (11,143)	Antagonistic (1,149)	
	Percentage by conduct of citizen			
Complainant, individual or group (5,837)*	46	43	16	42
Offender, individual or group (4,719)	31	31	71	34
All other† (3,383)	23	26	13	25
Total	100	100	100	100
	Percentage by role of citizen			
Complainant, individual or group (5,837)*	13	84	3	100
Offender, individual or group (4,719)	11	73	16	100
All other† (3,383)	11	85	4	100
Total	12	80	8	100

SOURCE: *Studies of Crime and Law Enforcement in Major Metropolitan Areas*, table 12.
*Figures in parentheses indicate number of encounters.
†Includes informants, bystanders, and sick or injured persons.

police is directed toward suspects or offenders. Indeed, all openly hostile or provocative behavior toward citizens occurred against offenders (see table 3.3). Uncivil behavior and misconduct of police toward citizens then is disproportionately directed against citizens the police or complainants define as "offenders," and the antagonistic behavior of citizens toward the police is disproportionately accounted for by offenders. The problem is to determine who initiated the uncivil behavior and what conditions prompted it.

Although more than three-fourths of all white police officers made prejudiced statements about Negroes, in actual encounters the police did not treat Negroes uncivilly more often than they did whites.[15] The results were the same for those cases where police officers assaulted citizens unnecessarily.[16] Both Negro and white policemen, moreover, were most likely to exercise force unduly against members of their *own* race. Given the racial composition of the populations each polices, it becomes apparent that, in the final analysis, race is not an issue in the unnecessary use of force by the police.[17]

Whether police use excessive force depends more upon conditions of the encounter than on racial prejudice. Seventy-eight percent of all instances where force was used unduly took place in police-controlled settings, such as the patrol car, the precinct station, or public places (primarily streets). Almost all victims of force were characterized as suspects or offenders. They were young, lower-class males from any racial or ethnic group.[18] Furthermore, most encounters were devoid of witnesses who would support the

15. Reiss, *Studies in Crime and Law Enforcement in Major Metropolitan Areas,* p. 66 and tables 10, 12, and 25.
16. Albert J. Reiss, Jr., "Police Brutality—Answers to Key Questions," *Trans-action* 5 (July-August 1968): 15–16.
17. Ibid., p. 16.
18. See Reiss, "Police Brutality," p. 17.

Table 3.3

Percentage Distributions for Conduct of Officer by Role of Citizen in 13,939 Encounters with the Police

Role of citizen	Conduct of police toward citizen						Total per-centage
	Personal (2,133)*	Civil (10,092)	Demeaning (645)	Authoritarian (655)	Threatening (311)	Hostile or provocative (103)	
Percentage by conduct of officer							
Complainant, individual or group (5,837)*	40	45	33	13	34	—	42
Offender, individual or group (4,719)	35	28	60	78	53	100	34
All other† (3,383)	25	27	7	9	13	—	24
Total	100	100	100	100	100	100	100
Percentage by role of citizen							
Complainant, individual or group (5,837)*	14	80	3	1	2	—	100
Offender, individual or group (4,719)	15	62	7	11	3	2	100
All other† (3,383)	16	81	1	1	1	—	100
Total	15	72	5	5	2	1	100

SOURCE: *Studies of Crime and Law Enforcement in Major Metropolitan Areas*, table 10.

*Figures in parentheses indicate number of encounters.

†Includes informants, bystanders, and sick or injured persons.

offender.[19] In general, persons officers regarded as being in a deviant offender role or who defied what the officer defines as his authority were the most likely victims of undue force. Thirty-nine percent openly defied authority by challenging the legitimacy of the police to exercise that authority, 9 percent physically resisted arrest, and 32 percent were persons in deviant offender roles, such as drunks, homosexuals, or addicts.[20] However, many instances where the citizen behaved antagonistically toward the police officer and many encounters with deviants did not involve uncivil conduct or misuse of force by the police. There appears to be yet another element involved in generating police misconduct toward citizens.

Chevigny's study of complaints to bureaus established by the New York Civil Liberties Union shows that 65 percent of all referred complaints and 71 percent of those authenticated through investigation involved some form of defiance of police authority.[21] Sixty-one percent of this defiance was verbal.[22] What an officer regards as an act defying his authority ranges considerably, from the simple act of recording an officer's badge number through physical resistance to arrest and open assault of the officer.

The right of police to assert authority where there is cause to believe a crime may have been committed is legitimated by legal institutions. Citizens usually respond to the assertion of police authority with high deference or civility, but in a substantial minority of encounters, at least one citizen does not. Officers frequently interpret any failure to grant deference as a challenge to their authority and make efforts to assert it. There is evidence that many situations that provoke police to use undue force closely resemble those

19. Ibid., pp. 19–20.
20. Ibid., p. 20.
21. Paul Chevigny, *Police Power: Police Abuses in New York City* (New York: Pantheon Books, 1969), p. 70.
22. Ibid., p. 71.

that give rise to assaults by private citizens. In both cases, the force is exerted in quick anger against real or imagined aggression.[23]

Subcultures and Misconduct

It is not clear whether this seeming necessity to assert police authority is provoked primarily by pressures from within the encounter, in that the assertion of authority is essential to make and sustain the arrest. As noted, an officer responds to a challenge to his authority by asserting authority. When the citizen acquiesces, there is no necessity for further attempts at assertion. Excessive force is exerted in a situation when it becomes unclear as to "who is in charge." In such cases, where challenges to police authority are at stake, the subculture becomes important because it demands that the officer show he is in charge. There are strong subcultural beliefs that the officer who ignores challenges from citizens loses the respect of the citizenry and makes it difficult for other officers to work in the precinct.[24] No challenge to authority, therefore, can go unmet until there is acquiescence to it. The police code prohibits "backing down." At the same time, many believe that citizens, particularly those from the lower classes, only understand and respect coercive authority. Therefore, threats to use coercive authority quickly yield to use of force.

Despite popular belief, deviants do not generally experience uncivil conduct and coercive authority from the police. This may be attributed to their ready compliance to police authority and their utility to the police. Their compliance stems either from their unwillingness to risk public exposure or from their dependence upon the police to con-

23. Ibid., p. 73.
24. John McNamara, "Uncertainties in Police Work," in David J. Bordua, ed., *The Police: Six Sociological Essays* (New York: John Wiley, 1967).

tinue to overlook their deviant practices. Furthermore, the position of deviants as part of the underlife of a community also serves to protect them from improper police practices, because they are an important source of information when the police wish to solve crimes or control that underlife. The exchange of information constrains the improper use of police authority.

The fact that lower-class males are disproportionally the targets of police misconduct, particularly in the undue use of force,[25] requires explanation. Males, of course, are more likely to aggress physically against authority than are women, and young males are more likely to than are older males. The literature on aggression also suggests that middle-class males respond to aggression against them with subtle forms of symbolic aggression, and they tend to postpone any resolution of the conflict. Lower-class males, by contrast, respond with physical forms of aggression and they attempt to resolve the conflict immediately. At the same time, the police seem to fear complaints from middle-class more than from lower-class males and are more likely to exercise restraint when challenged by middle-class men. The forms of aggression resorted to and responses to the assertion of authority, on the part of lower-class males, therefore, seem more likely to invite counteraggression by the police than do those of the middle-class male.

Observations of police behavior toward citizens indicate that, in the policing of everyday life, a small proportion of citizens experiences some form of police misconduct. Nevertheless, in the course of time, police misconduct cumulates over a population of citizens so that a sizeable minority of citizens experience police misconduct at one time or another. The striking fact is that relative to the actual incidence of police misconduct, the volume of complaints about it is low. No doubt, the opportunities citizens have to make com-

25. Reiss, "Police Brutality," p. 19; and Chevigny, chap. 12.

plaints and the confidence they place in organized forms of handling them affect the volume of complaints. But a major element in determining whether or not one complains seems to be the degree to which the conduct of the police is a matter of public as well as private concern in the society.

Three times within this century, the conduct of the police in the policing of everyday life has surfaced as a major public issue. Public concern in the past, as today, has been police conduct with respect to specific segments of the population. At the turn of the century, the misconduct of police toward the immigrant citizenry was a major issue in many American cities. Though precise data on the extent of police misconduct is lacking, the following reports by "inside" observers attest to its magnitude. Mr. Frank Moss, recently retired police commissioner of the City of New York wrote in 1901:

> For three years there has been through the courts and the streets a dreary procession of citizens with broken heads and bruised bodies against few of whom was violence needed to effect an arrest. Many of them had done nothing to deserve an arrest. In a majority of such cases no complaint was made. If the victim complains, his charge is generally dismissed. The police are practically above the law.[26]

Mr. William Gaynor of the Supreme Court of the State of New York wrote similarly in 1903:

> The last mayoralty election in the City of New York was probably decided by the large number of persons who during the previous four years had been unlawfully interfered with and oppressed by the police.[27]

26. Frank Moss, "National Danger from Police Corruption," *North American Review* 173 (October 1901): 470–80.
27. William J. Gaynor, "Lawlessness of the Police in New York," *North American Review* 176 (January 1903): 10–26.

The investigation of the Wickersham Commission in the Hoover Administration focused on police misconduct but with more emphasis on misconduct in the station than on the streets.[28] However, in the fifties and sixties, attention was again focused on misconduct[29] in the policing of ethnic minorities, particularly, this time, Negro and Spanish-speaking citizens.

Public concern about police conduct is less intent on fostering civil conduct than on prohibiting the police from using illegal means against citizens, particularly the illegal use of force. This concern is reflected in citizen complaints. Complaints about the undue use of force loom much larger among formal complaints of citizens than is actually the case for police misconduct toward citizens. Although demeaning conduct toward citizens is most common (based on observations of police and citizen encounters and surveys of citizens), formal complaints on such matters are proportionally small.

A study of complaints to the Philadelphia Police Advisory Board from 1958 to 1966 disclosed that 42 percent of all allegations were about "brutality," and a majority of these complaints arose in connection with an arrest. The remaining 58 percent alleged other illegal practices and, of these, 19 percent alleged illegal search, entry, or seizure of evidence; 22 percent, harassment; 9 percent other illegal means; and 8 percent more than one illegal means. The rate for the nonwhite population is estimated as greater than that for the white population. While only 39 percent of

28. National Commission on Law Observance and Enforcement, *Report on Lawlessness in Law Enforcement* (Washington, D.C.: USGPO, 1931).
29. U.S. Civil Rights Commission, *The 50 States Report* (Washington, D.C.: USGPO, 1961); and President's Commission on Law Enforcement and the Administration of Justice, *Task Force Report: The Police* (Washington, D.C.: USGPO, 1967), pp. 180–93; National Advisory Commission on Civil Disorders, *Report of the National Advisory Commission on Civil Disorders* (Washington, D.C.: USGPO, March 1, 1968), pp. 158–61.

all complaints about the undue use of force led citizens to seek some form of medical treatment, the extent of the force applied is not known.[30] During the short-lived Civilian Review Board in New York City, 51 percent of the 545 complaints alleged unnecessary force, 21 percent other illegal means and 28 percent discourtesy or ethnic slurs.[31] The Police Practices Project of the Defense and Education Fund, New York Civil Liberties Union, sought out complaints against the police with a view to litigation. Of the complaints received, 43 percent alleged assault by an officer, 29 percent false arrest, frame-up, or entrapment, 14 percent illegal search, and 11 percent other illegal means of investigation. Only 3 percent alleged discourtesy or demeaning behavior.[32]

Minority groups issue by far the largest numbers of complaints about police misconduct. For example, nonwhites in Philadelphia comprise about 27 percent of the population, yet they accounted for 63 percent of all complaints against the police.[33] Minority groups likewise accounted for 52 percent of all complaints lodged with the Civilian Complaint Review Board of New York City.[34] Chevigny reports that 40 percent of the complaints received by the Police Practices Project in New York were from Negroes or Puerto Ricans,[35] although the minority group composition for the New York population is lower. Perhaps more to the point, among Chevigny's complainants, 65 percent of those

30. Joseph D. Lohman et al., *The Police and the Community,* in President's Commission on Law Enforcement and the Administration of Justice (Washington, D.C.: USGPO, 1967), tables 9, 10 and 11.

31. Algernon D. Black, *The People and the Police* (New York: McGraw Hill, 1968), Appendix 4, pp. 242–43.

32. Chevigny, pp. 70–71 and Analytical Appendix, pp. 285–87.

33. Lohman et al., table 20.

34. Algernon Black, *The People and the Police,* Appendix 3, pp. 240–41.

35. Chevigny, p. 286.

alleging assault with, and without, arrest were Negroes or Puerto Ricans,[36] and 65 percent of the complaints alleging brutality received by the Philadelphia Police Advisory Board were from nonwhites.[37] Clearly, not only are allegations about police misconduct disproportionally received from minority group citizens, but the more serious allegations show an even greater discrepancy.

There are adequate motivational and organizational grounds for predicting that the more serious forms of police misconduct, such as the misuse of force, will generate a disproportionate volume of complaints. However, there must be some explanation for the fact that both firsthand reports by citizens in surveys and complaints to organizations are disproportionally received from minority group, particularly nonwhite, complainants, while the observation data show that class rather than race determines police misconduct.

This discrepancy could be ascribed to the possibility that police misconduct simply cumulates differently among racial and minority groups. However, it is more likely that these differences can be attributed to two other factors. First of all, observations have shown that white and nonwhite subjects are equally likely to experience police misconduct and the misuse of force. But, since nonwhites account for a disporportionate number of suspects or offenders, and this is the population group most vulnerable to police misconduct, complaints from the minorities are likely to be greatest. Secondly, the focus of public attention on police-minority relations and the emergence of organizations or groups that generate citizen complaints for minorities—encouraging minority group members to realize that someone speaks in their defense against the police— may be the most important factor of all. We are now in a period in American society where almost no one speaks for the lower-class white in his relations with the police while

36. Ibid.
37. Lohman et al., table 11.

much attention is focused on the lower-class black minority group member.

Officer Violations of The Law

Officers may be charged with violations of the law, as might ordinary citizens. Among the offenses it is commonly alleged officers commit are theft of money and goods, burglary of establishments, accepting bribes, shakedowns of offenders, offering false testimony, and participation in the illegal markets and practices of syndicated crime.

Officers can violate criminal statutes when on or off duty, but we shall consider only on-duty violations since our primary data were gathered through observation of officers on duty. Each observer spent an eight-hour tour of duty either on foot or in a car with one or more officers so they could not only observe how officers handled law-enforcement matters with citizens, but also how they behaved at all other times. Some officers, in some police precincts and cities, were observed more frequently than others. The effect of observation on limiting misconduct cannot be assessed accurately. It should be noted, however, that the highest rates of misconduct occurred where officers were observed least often.

Counting all felonies and misdemeanors, except assaults on citizens, the rate of criminal violation for officers observed committing one or more violations was 23.7 in City X, 21.9 in City Y, and 16.5 in City Z per 100 officers (table 3.4). Excluding any participation in syndicated crime, roughly 1 in 5 officers was observed in criminal violation of the law. There was some variation among the three cities in the crime patterns of police officers and the rate of violation.

The types of opportunities and situations that give rise to officers violating criminal statutes are relatively few. Opportunities arise principally in connection with the law-enforcement roles of officers, particularly in relationships with businesses and businessmen, policing traffic violators and

Table 3.4

Rate Per 100 Officers of Criminal Violations in Field Settings of Three Cities Reported by Observers or Officers or Alleged by Others

Type of crime or dishonest practice	City X		City Y		City Z	
	Number of officers*	Percentage of officers observed, self-reported, alleged	Number of officers*	Percentage of officers observed, self-reported, alleged	Number of officers*	Percentage of officers observed, self-reported, alleged
Officer accepts money to alter testimony report:						
Officer reports at trial stage	2	0.9	—	—	—	—
Officer reports intent for case	1	0.5	—	—	—	—
Officer reports for altering report	1	0.5	—	—	—	—
Subtotal	(4)	(1.9)	—	—	—	—
Officer carries weapon to leave on citizen:						
Observer saw weapon and officer reports this as reason	2	0.9	2	1.4	2	0.9
Subtotal	(2)	(0.9)	(2)	(1.4)	(2)	(0.9)
Officer receives money/merchandise on return of stolen property:						
Officer reports he has done	2	0.9	4	2.7	—	—
Subtotal	(2)	(0.9)	(4)	(2.7)	—	—

Table 3.4—Continued

Type of crime or dishonest practice	City X		City Y		City Z	
	Number of officers*	Percentage of officers observed, self-reported, alleged	Number of officers*	Percentage of officers observed, self-reported, alleged	Number of officers*	Percentage of officers observed, self-reported, alleged
Officer takes money/property from deviants:						
Observer saw	6	2.7	8	5.5	2	0.9
Officer reports he has done	4	1.8	—	—	—	—
Subtotal	(10)	(4.5)	(8)	(5.5)	(2)	(0.9)
Traffic violation: officer gives no citation and gets money:						
Observer definitely saw	4	1.8	—	—	2	0.9
Observer heard solicitation	2	0.9	—	—	—	—
Officer reports he does	3	1.4	—	—	—	—
Subtotal	(9)	(4.1)	(0)	(0)	(2)	(0.9)
Officer takes merchandise from burglarized establishment:						
Observer saw	3	1.4	3	2.0	—	—
Officer reports he has done	1	0.5	—	—	—	—
Alleged by merchant in observer's presence	2	0.9	—	—	—	—
Subtotal	(6)	(2.8)	(3)	(2.0)	—	—

Table 3.4—Continued

Type of crime or dishonest practice	City X		City Y		City Z	
	Number of officers*	Percentage of officers observed, self-reported, alleged	Number of officers*	Percentage of officers observed, self-reported, alleged	Number of officers*	Percentage of officers observed, self-reported, alleged
Officer receives money or merchandise from a business:†						
Observer saw merchandise taken and no citation or arrest	4	1.8	2	1.4	3	1.3
Observer saw only receipt of merchandise	11	5.0	6	4.1	15	6.5
Observer saw officers give special assistance for merchandise	2	0.9	6	4.1	10	4.3
Officer reports he does	2	0.9	1	0.7	4	1.7
Subtotal	(19)	(8.6)	(15)	(10.3)	(32)	(13.8)
Summary Officer Crimes/Practices:						
Total officers observed	32	14.5	29	18.5	34	14.8
Total officers by self-report	18	8.3	3	3.4	4	1.7
Total alleged against officers	2	0.9	—	—	—	—
Total officers—no crimes or dishonest practices	168	76.0	115	78.0	192	83.0
Total officers observed in study	220	100.0	147	100.0	230	100.0

SOURCE: Albert J. Reiss, Jr., Center for Research on Social Organization, University of Michigan, Project 947.

* An officer is counted only once with the offenses rank ordered in the table.

† Excluded are all free meals, discounts, small favors such as cigarettes or free drinks, and similar.

deviants, and controlling evidence from crimes (table 3.4). Obtaining money or merchandise illegally is the principal officer violation. A striking fact is that few officers were observed committing crimes against the residential property of citizens, although this may be a function of the fact that they usually were observed policing low-income residential areas. The major exception is the violation of criminal statutes by controlling evidence illegally, as by swearing false testimony or carrying additional weapons for the sole purpose of using them as evidence against citizens. These additional weapons were obtained from previous searches of the person, and are used as evidence against other citizens who were injured or killed, thereby buttressing the officer's argument that he injured or killed a citizen in self-defense.

The fact that criminal violations of the law by officers are restricted to relatively few types of offenses hints at the explanation for these offenses. The bulk of offenses committed by officers provide income supplements derived from exchange relationships. The price exacted by the officer provides something in exchange, generally exemption from the effect of the law. Given the relatively low remuneration of police officers, relative to their prestige and life style, the pressures to supplement income are considerable. Many police departments in the United States either prohibit moonlighting or severely restrict its practice to certain kinds of jobs. In any case, the "easy" money available to the officer with the low risk of sanctioning renders it a highly attractive form of income supplementation when contrasted with moonlighting. Though claims are easily exaggerated, some officers said they could earn as much from their violations as from their salary. Where either the pay-offs are regularized—as they often are for the protection offered illegal activity, or where there is considerable opportunity to exact money because the market is large, as is the case for shakedowns of traffic violators—and the pressure to balance income with expenditure is high, as it is for police officers, one should expect this pattern of violation of the criminal law. Gains are considerable relative to opportunity costs, assuming psychic income from exemplary conduct is not too great. Historically, political officials as well as police officers have been particularly vulnerable to this pattern of deviance.

Parenthetically, it might be noted that the effect of the criminal violations of officers still sanctions negatively the activity from which the financial gain is made. While the motorist who pays the police officer in exchange for exemption from official processing pays a cost below that which its sanctioning agents normally assess (the fine plus court costs and points), it nonetheless is a cost, and therefore a sanction. Indeed the police officer must make the cost of his sanction competitive.

The criminal violations of officers against the operation of the system of criminal justice is explained on altogether different grounds. The explanation of that misconduct lies in the officer subculture as a reaction to the system of punishment for police officers, a matter we shall turn to later.

A gray area of offending also exists. Many businessmen in a community engage in exchanges or practices with police officers that from the standpoint of the law could bring charges of bribery. A variety of such practices were uncovered in our observations of the police including almost daily free meals, drinks, or cigarettes, the profferment of gifts marking anniversaries and holidays, and discounts on purchases. Such practices are specifically prohibited by the rules and regulations of any police department and subject to disciplinary action if "officially" discovered.

Within each of the cities, one-third (31 percent) of all businessmen in wholesale or retail trade or business and repair services in the high-crime-rate areas openly acknowledged favors to policemen. Of those giving favors, 43 percent said they gave free merchandise, food or services to all policemen; the remainder did so at discount. When observers were present with officers during their eight-hour tour of duty, for almost 1 of every 3 of the 841 tours (31 percent), the officers did not pay for their meals. For the remaining cases, small discounts were common. Similarly many officers reported large discounts on purchases of durable goods. On most occasions, free goods or discounts are not solicited, largely because officers know well which businesses offer them and which do not. The informal police networks carry such information, obviating in most cases open solicitation. Presentation of self in uniform is all that is necessary to secure many benefits. These transactions are viewed as "favors" by the line and tacitly approved by their superiors.

The fact that mobility within police departments occurs almost exclusively by promotion from the line *within* a department makes line and staff officers subject to subversion by the line. They readily overlook practices and violations that are common among patrolmen either because they, themselves, engaged in them when they served as patrolmen or many of their friends did so. Not infrequently, when superior officers investigate or hear charges in disciplinary proceedings for men in the line, their judgment is subverted because they served with them. These facts—the absence of lateral mobility across police departments and mobility within them resting on promotion from the line—are a structural feature of American police departments that renders them vulnerable to many forms of internal subversion and jeopardizes their disinterest in personnel decisions and discipline. The classic separation of recruitment into staff and line and the use of civil-service examinations is designed to temper subversion in promotion. No such safeguard is built into the typical disciplinary investigation and hearing within the police department. Businessmen regard favors to police officers as guarantees that special attention may be given their business. Most such favors, therefore, do not occur as specific exchanges, characteristic of bribery and shakedowns. Rather, as Dalton points out for American businesses, they represent "favors due" that cannot be exchanged in the course of carrying out regular duties. Although it can be argued, as he notes, that people are being persuaded to violate their official duties by accepting such favors, it can equally be argued that they contribute to the carrying out of official duties.[38] Thus, it is the duty of the police to protect business establishments in the community. Indeed, since businesses are highly vulnerable to criminal activity in many areas, special attention may even be officially approved. In Detroit and Chicago, as in some other large American cities, the police department may even provide a police escort at closing time so that businessmen may safely deposit their daily receipts at a bank. Such attention, though not officially acknowledged by either party as payment can be recognized through favors. For the police, then, as for workers and officials in corporations, favors often are unofficial rewards for regular duties.[39]

Such exchanges may not afford businesses the protection anticipated. Within each of the police precincts a sample of businesses was investigated to determine whether personal relationships with police officers affects a business's capacity to cope with crime against it. Examining the businesses in 1966 and 1968, it was found that businesses with personal links to police officers in 1966 maintained them in 1968. However, these personal relationships were totally ineffective in reducing the level of crime against these businesses. Thus, the high degree of personal links that businesses have with the police cannot be explained by any added benefits to the organization in meeting its crime problems.[40]

38. Melville Dalton, *Men Who Manage* (New York: John Wiley, 1966), p. 200.
39. For an extended discussion of these practices in American businesses, see Dalton, chap. 7.
40. See Howard Aldrich, "Organizations in a Hostile Environment: A Panel Study of Small Businesses in Three Cities" (Ph.D. diss., The University of Michigan, 1969), pp. 98–99.

Infractions of Departmental Rules and Regulations

Typically, all but the smaller police departments in the United States have a Police Manual setting forth the rules and regulations of the department and prescribing what is duty and what is right or proper conduct. In addition, the chief may issue orders that define and specify duty and conduct. Much as in the military, larger departments may even require officers to acknowledge in writing that they have read the order.

Although the extent to which duty and conduct is specified varies across departments, commonly any police officer is held responsible for civil deportment at all times and forbidden to engage in many acts permitted ordinary citizens both on and off duty. A police officer, for instance, is not allowed to drink intoxicating liquor on duty and when off duty not to an extent that would render him unfit for immediate duty. Similarly, he is required to pay promptly all debts and obligations and must not solicit or make contributions for political purposes.[41]

During our observation of the police, an attempt was made to record infractions of rules that the department considered serious violations. They include drinking and sleeping while on duty, neglect of duty by unauthorized time away from duty for other than police matters, and falsification of information on police matters.

Given the fact that 38 percent of all Negro and 46 percent of all white officers were observed during only one eight-hour tour of duty the observed rate of rule infraction was high. Roughly 4 in every 10 officers were observed in one of the more serious violations of rules (table 3.5). There was considerable variation in rules infractions among the cities;

41. See, for example, *Police Manual: Containing the Rules and Regulations of the Metropolitan Police Department of the City of St. Louis, Missouri*, Board of Police Commissioners (December 1964), esp., Rule 3 and Rule 7, all secs.

Table 3.5

Rate Per 100 Officers of Infractions of Police Department Rules Observed in Field Settings of Two Police Precincts in Each of Three Cities, by Race of Officer

Type of rule infraction by police district*	City X Officers in infractions†				City Y Officers in infractions†				City Z Officers in infractions†			
	Number		Rate		Number		Rate		Number		Rate	
	W	NW	W	NW	W	NW	W	NW	W	NW	W	NW
Drinking on duty												
District A	3	x	3.3	x	3	x	5.2	x	4	—	9.1	—
District B	2	4	2.1	11.5	9	—	11.1	—	15	1	25.4	11.1
Subtotal, both	(5)	(4)	(3.2)	(11.5)	(12)	(—)	(8.6)	(—)	(19)	(1)	(18.4)	(6.7)
Sleeping on duty												
District A	1	x	1.1	x	7	x	12.1	x	—	—	—	—
District B	9	6	9.5	17.1	21	1	25.9	14.3	10	—	16.9	—
Subtotal, both	(10)	(6)	(6.5)	(17.1)	(28)	(1)	(20.0)	(14.3)	(10)	(—)	(9.7)	(—)
Neglect of duty												
District A	2	x	2.2	x	15	x	25.8	x	5	—	11.4	—
District B	8	2	8.4	5.7	10	2	12.3	28.5	2	—	3.4	—
Subtotal, both	(10)	(2)	(6.5)	(5.7)	(25)	(2)	(17.9)	(28.5)	(7)	(—)	(6.8)	(—)
Falsification of reports												
District A	2	x	2.2	x	1	x	1.7	x	—	—	—	—
District B	2	2	2.1	5.7	—	—	—	—	1	—	1.7	—
Subtotal, both	(4)	(2)	(2.6)	(5.7)	(1)	(—)	(0.7)	(—)	(1)	(—)	(1.0)	(—)

Table 3.5—Continued

| Type of rule infraction by police district* | City X Officers in infractions† | | | | City Y Officers in infractions† | | | | City Z Officers in infractions† | | | |
| | Number | | Rate | | Number | | Rate | | Number | | Rate | |
	W	NW	W	NW	W	NW	W	NW	W	NW	W	NW
Other major infractions‡												
District A	—	x	—	x	—	x	—	x	2	—	4.5	—
District B	1	—	1.1	—					—	—	—	—
Subtotal, both	(1)	(—)	(0.6)	(—)	(—)	(—)	(—)	(—)	(2)	(—)	(1.9)	(—)
ALL IN INFRACTIONS												
District A	8	x	8.9	x	26	x	44.8	x	11	—	25.0	—
District B	22	14	23.1	40.0	40	3	49.3	42.8	28	1	47.4	11.1
Total, both	(30)	(14)	(18.9)	(40.0)	(66)	(3)	(47.1)	(42.8)	(39)	(1)	(37.9)	(6.7)
ALL NOT IN INFRACTIONS												
District A	82	x	91.1	x	32	x	55.2	x	33	6	75.0	100.0
District B	73	21	76.9	60.0	42	4	51.7	57.1	31	8	52.6	88.9
Total, both	(155)	(21)	(81.1)	(60.0)	(74)	(4)	(52.9)	(57.1)	(64)	(14)	(62.1)	(93.3)

SOURCE: Albert J. Reiss, Jr., Center for Research on Social Organization, University of Michigan, Project 947.
NOTE: W = White; NW = Nonwhite. The letter x as a column entry indicates no nonwhite officers.

*District A has a higher proportion of white than nonwhite population with District B the reverse; all are high-crime-rate precincts in the three cities.

†An officer is counted only once for the "most serious" infraction as rank ordered in the table.

‡Includes "playing the numbers" or other gambling while on duty and the use of patrol car for "immoral" purposes.

drinking on duty was observed for only 4 of every 100 officers in City X, but for 18 of every 100 in City Z. Similarly,
sleeping while on duty was observed for 2 of every 100 officers in City Y, but for less than half that in City X. Neglect
of duty also was very high in City Y compared with other
cities. There likewise was considerable variation in the rate
of rules violations by race composition of the precinct and
the race of officer, both within and among cities. White officers assigned to nonwhite precincts had higher rates of rules
violations than those in white precincts. In City X, with the
highest proportion of nonwhite officers, the rate of infraction
was highest for nonwhite officers.

How, then, is one to account for officers violating the
more serious rules and regulations of the police department? Their rate of infraction seems to be a function of two
major factors related to the organization of command and
control within the department: the quality of supervision of
line officers and the transfer policies of the department. City
rates and precinct rates are generally lower where supervision is effective. Supervision has a particularly strong effect
on such infractions as sleeping on duty, drinking on duty,
and neglect of duty. Rule infraction is lowest where the command is most centralized and where supervision is exercised
by men in the field.

Job assignment and transfer within police departments
generally are organized so that officers with the least training
and experience are assigned to the highest crime-rate precincts. Officers with the poorest records of performance likewise are transferred to these areas. In American cities today,
such police precincts often are nonwhite. These policies and
practices of assignment and transfer were especially evident
in City Y where officers in the nonwhite area openly acknowledged they were assigned there because "there was
no place else to be sent." Two types of deviant officers were
so assigned: those who basically did excellent police work
but were against the system, taking every opportunity to

show their disregard for it, and those who were both poor police officers and had been sanctioned previously for infractions of rules. Slum police precinct stations, not unlike slum schools, collect the "rejects" of the system. A transfer practice whereby any local commander may veto reassignment is especially vulnerable to this form of subversion, since generally the commander permits only the poorer quality officers to transfer from his command (unless, of course, he has a "corrupt" command). These reasons suggest that the rate of officer deviance is higher among those assigned to high-crime-rate areas than among others.

A department's official reports reveal little about officer infractions of the law and the rules and regulations of police departments. Unlike the crime statistics they publish for offenders, police departments no longer publish charges against officers and the dispositions made of them. This is in sharp contrast to the nineteenth century when police departments commonly published the officer's name as well as the charge and the disposition made of it.

This latter form of accountability in reporting persisted until well into the twentieth century when such information disappeared altogether from any of the published reports. Since such reports were made for the New York City Police Department when it had more than 10,000 men, its disappearance seems to have little relationship to any growth in size of United States police departments; only two departments today have more than 10,000 officers. Rather, its disappearance seems more closely linked to the growth of bureaucratic and legal rationalization of disciplinary proceedings, which protect the identity of officers and restrict the practice of reporting for offenses. The failure of many police departments to publish even summary statistics, however, probably results from a decline in the use of the annual report of any municipal agency as an instrument of accountability and its rise as an instrument of public relations.

A very recent study by Bernard Cohen of the Rand Institute of New York City on how the New York City Police Department handles charges of officer misconduct provides some support for all of our findings on officer misconduct. For the cohort of 1,915 police officers who entered the department in 1957, there were 2,137 allegations of misconduct from 1957 to 1968. Almost 60 percent of the men who became patrolmen in 1957 received at least one complaint against them during their first decade of service. Complaints were more common against black officers (80 percent) than against white officers (57 percent). Of the 2,137 complaints, 9.5 percent were criminal charges, 25.3 percent accused an officer of abusing a citizen, and 64.2 percent cited violation of department rules such as moonlighting or sleeping on duty.[42]

There is good reason to assume that estimates of the rate of officers' offenses, based on complaints received by official police agencies, are very low. The fact that 60 percent of the officers in the department received at least one such complaint against them during the decade suggests high annual rates of offending. It is also probable that the rate of officer offenses, when observed over a short period of time is substantially below the true rate. Were one to extrapolate from either the Reiss or Cohen study, the conclusion seems inescapable that during any year a substantial minority of all police officers violate the criminal law, a majority misbehave toward citizens in an encounter, and most engage in serious violations of the rules and regulations of the department. Indeed, if one examines citizen allegations of mistreatment by police officers, it becomes apparent that these offenses often fall under criminal statutes of assault and battery. A majority of officers in this sense violate the criminal statutes.

42. Bernard Cohen, *The Police Internal Administration of Justice in New York City* (New York: The Rand Institute of New York City, November 1970), sec. 6 and Appendix C.

Explaining the Deviance of Officers

We have tried to show how the deviant conduct of officers may arise based on the structure and organization of police work as well as police culture. We have shown that a substantial proportion of officers have engaged in one or more forms of deviant conduct and the annual rates of offending may be high. Yet, what standard does one use to determine whether the rate of offending by officers is high or low?

This is an important question, because the police encounter in their work much pressure and opportunity from offenders as well as legitimate and illegitimate organized interests to deviate from laws and rules governing conduct. Even in such minor matters as traffic violations, the conforming citizen wants a pass, expects special consideration, and often is willing to pay an officer to ignore the matter. Businessmen wanting to violate ordinances for closing hours or serving customers or wishing profit from illegal markets are willing to offer special consideration in return for the opportunity to do business as they wish. In short, there is ample opportunity for subversion of any and all officers.

All officers are, to a large extent, exempt from law enforcement. This fact, combined with the pressures on an officer to deviate in many situations make each crime opportunity for him a more likely criminal event. Bearing this in mind, the question is not, what makes officers violate the law, but what protects officers from deviating more often than we have observed?

The likelihood of an officer accepting illegal exchanges is increased when such practices are institutionalized and legitimated by the police subculture and organization. We found that traffic bribes were most common in the city where they had long been an institutionalized form of exchange between police and citizens. The exchange became legitimated. At the same time, however, an officer takes a certain risk in making the exchange. Thus, he generally will not do so in the presence of witnesses or when detection is likely. A further element influencing officer involvement in such exchanges is the degree to which these illegal practices are organized, as in a system of exchange with organized crime. Typical of such exchanges is that they get organized as an economy where rewards are distributed on a routine basis.

What may be most pertinent here is the legitimacy that attaches to the exchange. To deviate on one's own is to be a criminal, but where the offense is consensual, not only is there mutual implication in the offense, and therefore minimization of risk, but the offense is also easily legitimized. For an officer to share in a payment from illegal gambling is accepted, but for an officer to burglarize an establishment is to step beyond the bounds of what is legitimate. Deviation, we observe, often is *shared* with fellow officers, providing peer support to each. Furthermore, rules infractions, such as drinking or sleeping on duty, are participated in by several officers at a time, although when this is not the case, they may rely on the subculture to protect them. No doubt, image protection operates here as well, but the punishment system is important, a matter we shall turn to later. To suggest, of course, that the only pressures against deviance are these is to scant the fact that officers do commit themselves to uphold a moral order. Some psychic investment is made in exemplary conduct.

Summary

Police standards and conduct are based primarily on five sources: (1) subversion by the citizenry; (2) the input-output system, particularly where the police lack control over final outcomes; (3) the quality of citizen behavior toward the police; (4) the existence of a dispersed command that does not lend itself to close supervision; and (5) legitimation by the police subculture and shared participation in deviance. In the long run, we have had only one solution to the problem of conformity to standards for occupations that are dispersed in work situations, their professionalization. Lest anyone assume that professionalization is a uniquely satisfactory solution, he must be reminded that charges of professional malpractice are not uncommon. In our legal system, such charges can on occasion reach even to the highest levels of our appellate system, the United States Supreme Court.[43]

43. See the case not only of Justice Abraham Fortas, but also those of nominees for judicial vacancies.

IV

TOWARD A CIVIL POLICE

Evidence has been presented indicating that citizen attitudes and expectations about the police and police service affect whether or not they call the police. When American citizens call the police, generally they do so less from a sense of civic duty than from an expectation of personal gain. However, it is their willingness to live up to an obligation to mobilize the police for violations of the law, whether against themselves, others, or the public order, that is a major element in maintaining a civil society. It mirrors their acceptance of responsibility for and to the whole society. A police force that works mainly by responding to citizen requests for police service is more consistent with a civil society then is one that relies mainly on police initiative. The willingness of citizens to commit their adversary relations to the legal system, including the system of law enforcement, is an additional element, since a civil society is one that operates through the rule of law. Since civility is born of trust, the extent of trust and confidence the police and public have in one another is also of utmost importance for a civil society.

Today, American society is divided on issues of law, public order, and justice. Faced with political pressures that hold crime and violence to be major problems, the executive branch of the federal government named a series of commissions in the 1960s to investigate crime, law enforcement and criminal justice, civil disorders, violence in American life, and campus unrest. The work of these commissions focused on what is known about the causes of crime, disorder, and violence, and the failure of all of our systems, not only those of law enforcement and criminal justice, to successfully deal with these problems. While these are important matters, more fundamental questions were neglected. The commissions raised questions such as: What makes men violent in their relations with one another? How can one reduce violence? What makes men racist? How can one reduce racism? While these are important questions, more fundamental ones were neglected: What makes men civil in their relations with one another? How can one enhance civility among them? How does one develop a civilized society?

At the outset, let me clarify what is meant by civility. *Civility* exists when men behave in ordinary affairs with a sense of concern and responsibility for the interests of others. Outwardly, their demeanor is marked by politeness. The sociologist Edward Shils adds that civility is the virtue of the citizen, not that of the hero or private man. It is marked by the sense of responsibility for and to the entire society and a general acceptance of the rules that are valid within it.[1] A civilized society is not necessarily one of high culture, but rather one where there is a wide distribution of civility. Such a society is more likely to insist upon minimum rather than maximum standards of conduct in human affairs out of regard for and balancing individual and collective interests. Above all, such a society requires that men behave in everydays life with a civil disposition.

So far as civil relations between the police and the public are concerned, the following conditions must prevail: (1) that citizens be civil in their relations with one another, including the police; (2) that citizens grant legitimacy to police authority and respect their legal intervention in the affairs of

1. Edward A. Shils, "The Theory of Mass Society," *Diogenes* 39 (1962): 56.

men; (3) that the police be accountable to civil authority and the citizen protected from police tyranny.

Legitimacy in the Exercise of Police Authority

By custom and at law in America, the intervention of the police in the affairs of men is regarded as legitimate provided it is done legally. Police are even granted the right to use violence toward citizens if it is necessary to protect their own lives, essential to the arrest of a felon, or necessary to maintain public order. Maintaining the legitimacy of police authority, in practice, depends, however, upon several other elements.

The way police *exercise* their authority in encounters with citizens is important in maintaining its legitimacy. The legal exercise of police authority reinforces the right of police to use it, while its illegal exercise undermines the broader acceptance of the authority as legitimate. Clearly, the police do not always exercise their authority in legal ways, especially toward members of the lower classes, minorities, and deviant groups. When the police lack broad acceptance of their authority, they must find a way to legitimate their authority.

Citizens may also grant legitimacy to police authority by showing *deference* toward its legal exercise. Clearly, if citizens fail to grant deference, the police must justify their authority as they intervene in the affairs of citizens.

The use of the police to uphold the law and maintain public order may itself become a threat to public acceptance of police authority as legitimate. This is especially true when the police are used to control private morality and public dissent. The exercise of police discretion in defining behavior as disorderly conduct, criminal trespass, or a breach of the peace, for example, may undermine police authority, because the police are responsible for making such decisions on controversial issues. The policing of vice erodes police authority when police impose a standard that is unpopular with a substantial segment of the local community. Selective enforcement of unpopular laws invariably is seen as the arbitrary exercise of authority. The policing of vice also tends to undermine police authority because it leaves police vulnerable to subversion through the corruption of police conduct; a corrupt police hardly can lay claim to legitimacy of moral authority.

Matters involving dissent particularly corrode police authority because the participants tend to redirect their hostility against political authority onto the police.[2] The police are especially vulnerable to this displacement of hostility when these dissenters are challenging the legitimacy of authority to make decisions. The police who can do so little about changing the status quo become the symbols of all that is the status quo. Indeed, local communities bear much of the burden of controversy in the larger society. Regardless of the sources of dissent, it commonly manifests itself in challenges to local institutions and organizations, and the responsibility for controlling dissenters thereby falls upon the local police.[3]

The legitimacy of police authority also may be challenged within the legal system, when the constitutionality of police practices is questioned. When citizen rights are extended, police rights often are curtailed, and vice versa. The right of the police to process citizens as suspicious persons, to search them or their property, to stop and question them, or to detain them on open charges, all represent challenges as to what is the legitimate exercise of police power.

The police are in a paradoxical position in maintaining the

2. See Allan Silver, "The Demand for Order in Civil Society," in David Bordua, ed., The Police: Six Sociological Essays (New York: John Wiley, 1967), pp. 12–24.

3. See Albert J. Reiss, Jr., "Some Sociological Issues about American Communities," in Talcott Parsons, ed., American Sociology: Perspectives, Problems, Methods (New York: Basic Books, 1968), pp. 66–73.

legitimacy of their authority in the policing of everyday life. In practice, their power to decide whether they should intervene in the affairs of citizens is enormously circumscribed. They are expected to exercise very little discretion in deciding whether to respond to citizen requests to intervene in situations and almost none when organizations that lay special claim to authority request that police intervene in maintaining the public peace. The recent debates about police on college campuses are illustrative. They centered on the question: "Should the police be *allowed* to come on campus?" I never heard the question raised: "Should the police *refuse* to come on a college campus, if requested to do so?" All that the police are expected to decide when they are requested to intervene is *how* to do so, not whether or not they should.

While the police have little power to decide whether to intervene when requested to do so, they nonetheless are held responsible for the *act* of intervention, both by those who request they intervene and by those they are expected to police. Needless to say, the concept of responsibility for intervention is often not the same for all parties. The necessity to intervene in the affairs of citizens when coupled with a dependence upon citizen willingness to grant legitimacy to that intervention creates a special problem for the exercise of police authority. The police must *establish their right to intervene* when legitimacy is not granted.

Citizens readily grant legitimacy for much of the policing of everyday life. Little problem exists for the police when citizens grant legitimacy to their intervention even when they do not have the legal right to intervene. The citizen who calls the police because he has been victimized by a crime automatically grants legitimacy to the police and ordinarily behaves with deference or civility toward them.

It is difficult for police to determine *how* to establish their right to intervene and carry out duty when citizens fail to grant that right, especially when refusal is accompanied by open aggression against the police. A crowd of students yelling "fascist pigs" or an offender resisting arrest do more than fail to show deference: they openly challenge the right to exercise authority.

Theoretically, there are several options when the legitimacy of police intervention is challenged. The first is to refuse to exercise the legal right to intervene in any situation. The ministerial right of police discretion in such matters is rarely challenged within the legal system. Yet, both the police and the public increasingly expect that when the police are called, they will come, and when they come, they will not withdraw until they have carried out their duty. Moreover, citizens and the public, as well as legal officers, may demand that the police intervene precisely when legitimacy is not granted. Generally, the police are unlikely to exercise this option to withdraw from an encounter when their right to intervene is challenged, particularly if the complainant insists upon their presence.

A second option is to set clear standards about how police authority is to be exercised when it is challenged in encounters with citizens. Generally legislators have been reluctant to restrict even the conditions under which the police may use deadly force, though some states now restrict its use to felonies. Political officers and police officials display a similar reluctance to set clear standards for the exercise of coercive authority. Hence, the individual officer must use his own discretion to determine whether and how to exercise his legal right in an encounter.

Despite the reluctance of others to set official standards for the exercise of police authority when it is challenged, the formal and informal training of officers teaches procedures for handling citizens when authority is challenged. Officers learn primarily through experience on the job, seeing how techniques such as rational argument, persuasion, humor, and actual force are practiced by older officers to control challenges to authority. Our studies of the police show that officers handle challenges to authority in all of these ways.

Indeed, they most commonly resort to means other than the exercise of physical force or threats to use it.

Research on aggression toward authority tells us that, unless inhibited, the most common response to aggression is counteraggression. And, furthermore, that counteraggression depends upon the subjective assessment individuals make about aggression against them, particularly whether or not they are threatened by it.

What we do know about how American police respond to aggression? All of the research on them shows that they have a high investment in wanting citizens to show deference to police authority and they are threatened by any failure to grant that deference. They are more likely to be punitive when deference is withheld than when it is granted.

Investment in securing deference is not peculiar to the police. It is common to most relationships involving authority. In many instances, when authority is challenged, it is not uncommon for one party to coerce deference by delegating enforcement to someone else. Commonly, when citizens are unable to secure deference toward their own authority, particularly if someone aggresses against it, they ask the police to intervene. Professionals when faced with unruly clients commonly call the police. The record of principals and teachers in city schools in the 1960s amply demonstrates the problem that professionals may have in obtaining and maintaining deference to their authority.

Police expectations regarding deference from citizens are strongly reinforced by their experiences with officials in the criminal-justice system. Nowhere in the police officer's experience is deference required more than in the courtroom. No one punishes even minor threats to deference more than judges, who expect everyone, including lawyers, to show deference toward their authority. Cases of lawyers being cited for contempt of judicial authority are not uncommon. Judges, in fact, surround themselves with police of their own. When they cannot secure deference, they summon these police. A judge who cannot maintain order in the court by sheer weight of *his* authority may, for example, first issue orders for silence, and then for contempt. Failing this, he may issue orders to detain or to clear the court, and he fully expects that the bailiffs or police will exercise *their* authority to do so.

Since police realize they cannot count on citizen support of their authority they commonly enter encounters with citizens by *asserting* their authority by "taking charge." Having asserted authority, they must seek to maintain it, if necessary, by force. Whether an officer will use force depends both upon department policy and the discretion of the officer. Most of the time, police officers operate in a dispersed command situation without supervision. The decision to use force, therefore, usually rests entirely with the individual officer.

The decision of an individual officer to exercise force in a situation is based not simply on his failure to secure deference to his authority but also on his assessment of the effect the use of force will have in a situation. Police officers, like the line in the army,[4] are reluctant to use force if their own safety cannot be guaranteed. Our police observation studies show that line officers will not carry out their legitimate right to arrest or enforce an arrest if they are confronted with hostile bystanders in sizeable numbers. The failure of officers to police looting in riots or to use force in policing disorders results from their subjective assessments of the personal risks involved.

Reciprocity and Civility

Again, the behavior of the police is based upon a relationship with citizens. In America, conflict often arises over expectations of each group, concerning its treatment by the

4. Charles C. Moskos, Jr., "A Sociologist Appraises the G.I.," *The New York Times Magazine* (September 24, 1967): pp. 32 ff.

other. Our surveys show that the police want citizens to grant them deference and citizens want the police to treat them as persons rather than cases.[5] Yet we also find that, in their transactions, each, for the most part, behaves toward the other in a civil fashion. However, neither is *satisfied* with this civility. Officers want more than civility; they want deference. And, citizens finding this civility at best bureaucratic and therefore somewhat demeaning, would prefer the officer to show personal involvement with their problem and offer individual attention.[6]

Since police and citizen relations are necessarily problematic when the citizens' violations of the law are at stake, to require that an officer show personal involvement seems a particularly stringent requirement. Indeed, the core element in professionalization of relations with clients is a requirement that the practitioner disengage himself from personal involvement with the client. Disengagement is an essential element in maintaining the objectivity so essential to the proper exercise of professional discretion.

Both the bureaucratic and the professional models for handling clients are viewed with skepticism and hostility by many clients, because from their perspective, both models place the case rather than the person at the core of the practice. The bureaucracy decides the case according to rules. The discretion exercised as to which rule applies is under no circumstances to rest in a personal relationship (unless it be by rule!). Professional discretion is based on knowledge and standards about the client's problems, and while professionals may take account of client interests, they must do so without becoming personally involved. The problem for the professional and the bureaucrat, and above all, the pro-

5. Albert J. Reiss, Jr., in President's Commission on Law Enforcement and the Administration of Justice, *Studies in Crime and Law Enforcement in Major Metropolitan Areas,* Field Surveys III, vol. 2, sec. 1 (Washington, D.C.: USGPO, 1967), pp. 57–60; and sec. 2, pp. 71–94.
6. Ibid., secs. 1 and 2.

fessional in the bureaucracy, however, is to satisfy the client as well as consider his interests. Therefore, a human-relations approach to handling clients is followed in professional and bureaucratic settings. But, even this type of technique often focuses more on the practitioner, the practice, and the bureaucracy than on the client. Clients come to perceive themselves as "manipulated," charging that the techniques employed are not based on a genuine interest in them as persons.

A civil and a democratic society requires reciprocity if frequent breakdowns in citizen and police relations are to be avoided. Civility must be met with civility. This has more or less been the case in police and citizen relationships in England and the Scandinavian countries where relations between the citizens and their police are governed more by custom than by legality.[7] The maintenance of a reciprocity system depends to a high degree on the *reinforcement* of reciprocity in both citizen and police systems.

I have already tried to suggest that reciprocity necessarily breaks down when police authority is challenged and thereby the citizen-police relationship enters a cycle where conflict may escalate. Each may progressively move toward the exercise of coercive authority, with threats of violence followed by the use of force. Clearly, how much force either the police or citizens have in their possession is important. An unarmed police cannot use armed force. An unarmed police depends, of course, upon an unarmed citizenry.

More is at issue in reciprocity than the use of force. Any reciprocating system requires that the sanctioning of parties for failing to reciprocate must be symmetrical, and any asymmetry in enforcement generally leads to a breakdown of the system. For citizens this means that, if the police are not neg-

7. See Michael Banton, *The Police and the Community* (London: *Tavistock* Publications, 1964), chaps. 4, 6, and 9; and T. A. Critchley, *A History of Police in England and Wales, 900–1966* (London: Constable, 1967), pp. 319–22.

atively sanctioned for incivility and the improper use of authority, citizens will come to behave uncivilly toward them. And, likewise, if citizens are not sanctioned negatively for incivility and use of force against the police and other citizens, the system will degenerate into the arbitrary use of force by the police. In short, much depends not only upon reciprocity of expectations but also reciprocity in sanctions for deviations from the norm of civility.

Comparison of American society with some other democratic societies in the sanctioning of violence by police and citizens is instructive. In England and Scandinavia, the use of violence is sanctioned negatively more or less universally in the society.[8] If anything, in police and citizen relations, it is more serious for the citizen to behave with violence toward the police than the other way around, because the police may legitimately use force. Evidence from English courts regarding charges of citizen violence toward the police shows that such behavior is severely punished.[9]

There is considerable evidence that the sanctioning of violence is not treated as problematic in our criminal-justice system, except in the controversy over capital punishment. The level of concern over police and citizen violence toward one another may be high, as it was in the late 1960s in the United States, where it culminated in the appointment of a commission to investigate the causes and prevention of violence. Nonetheless there is little evidence in any of the staff reports or the commission report of concern for how violence is sanctioned and handled in the system of criminal justice.[10]

What evidence we have on how police organizations sanction misconduct by police toward citizens shows that the police are unlikely to punish officers charged by citizens with

8. Nils Christie, "Changes in Penal Values," *Scandinavian Studies in Criminology* 2 (1968): 161–72.
9. Royal Commission on the Police, *Final Report* (London: HMSO, 1962).
10. See the *Progress Report to the President* and *Task Force Reports,* vols. 1–13 (Washington, D.C.: USGPO, 1969–70).

misconduct. The Rand Institute study of the way that the
New York City Police Department dealt with 541 allegations
of police misconduct toward citizens shows that 85 percent
of the complaints were dismissed or filed. Warnings, repri-
mands, and conciliation characterized all but 1 percent of
the remaining 15 percent. Only one policeman received a
major fine, a penalty that meant the loss of 10 days pay or
more.[11] The prosecutors and courts are similarly unlikely to
regard police misconduct toward citizens as serious, preferring not to risk suits for civil damages against the city or to
jeopardize the conviction of citizens.[12]

Nor is there much evidence that police, prosecutors, or
judges treat the violence of citizens toward one another seriously, particularly when it occurs among persons known to
each other. Treating the family altercation as a civil matter
may itself contribute to the escalation of violence in the system. Moreover, to argue that violence may be cultural and
therefore condoned is to create a climate for incivility.

The real problem is how can a civil society be established?
I do not propose to discuss this broad problem, but only to
state a few implications for citizen and police relations in
the absence of such a society. I have already indicated that
when a system does not severely sanction citizens *and* police
for incivility toward one another, the system degenerates
into the arbitrary use of force by the police. In that connection, I should point out that much training of the police in
the area of human relations, in my judgment, seems at best
misguided. It is not uncommon in such programs to try to
train the police to accept incivility with indifference. I submit that in a civil society no one should be trained or paid to
accept incivility; to accept invectives that begin with

11. Bernard Cohen, *The Police Internal Administration of Justice in
New York City* (New York: The Rand Institute of New York City,
November 1970), pp. 27–28.
12. Paul Chevigny, *Police Power: Police Abuses in New York City*
(New York: Pantheon Books, 1969).

"mother" or animal names. That is not to say that the police cannot be disciplined and trained to deal in a civil fashion with citizens who behave with incivility. They must! But failure to sanction incivility toward the police on the grounds that the police should expect, and therefore accept it, is to lay the ground for even less civility of citizens toward the police and for the police to respond in kind when opportunity presents itself.

Equally important for a civil society is the granting of legitimacy to the police in their intervention. American society is more inhospitable toward its police than most societies, and this is most evident in the virulent forms this inhospitality can take in the university.[13] Even arming students can be accepted by the academy more readily than calling in the police. The degree to which a society opts to entrust order to its police is always at issue. In the long run, both the necessity to rely upon police intervention to establish orderly relations among men, and the civility of police in doing so, depends upon the civility of the citizenry and their trust in a civil police.

Civic Accountability of the Police

Civil relations between citizens and the police depend in part upon the confidence citizens have that the police will behave in a civil fashion. Confidence is enhanced when people are convinced that others are accountable to them. Historically, police departments have been accountable to citizens primarily through their accountability to political authority.

A crucial feature of the accountability of police organizations in modern democratic societies is the political protection it affords citizens from police tyranny. Citizens are in a paradoxical situation before a government and its police.

13. S. M. Lipset, "Why Cops Hate Liberals—and Vice Versa," *The Atlantic* (March 1969), pp. 76–83.

On the one hand, they are vulnerable to state tyranny that is enforced through police organization, i.e., a "police state." On the other hand, they are vulnerable to police tyranny when state authority is unable to directly control or hold police organizations accountable.

The organizational form that is taken by any system of accountability bears an important relationship to this paradox. The vulnerability of citizens to state tyranny has led some societies to delegate authority for policing everyday life to local government so that the police will be *accountable to local authority*. Local police systems in the United States have been inaccessible to control by the centralized state and federal bureaucracies, because their budgets are based on local revenues and they are accountable to the central bureaucracies only through the legal system. This safeguard against state tyranny, by organizing police on a local community basis, leaves the citizen more vulnerable to local police tyranny, since the state's right and opportunity to intervene is limited.

Furthermore, local control of a police system, leaves the police open to partisanship, with strong pressures to control them emanating from local political elites and interest groups. The creation of metropolitan police forces in mid-nineteenth-century America brought with it a measure of bureaucratization of police service. However, for much of that century, the accountability of the police rested in the feudal relations of city ward politics and the spoils system. Policemen were without tenure and their recruitment and promotion depended upon satisfying local politicians and officials. Local police precinct commanders were as accountable to ward leaders as they were to the chief.

The "good government" movement rebelled against this spoils system and introduced the merit system of appointment to insure quality and responsibility for service by tenure rather than by political fealty. Many offices, such as that of the police chief were removed from direct election and made appointive on the theory that accountability to the electorate would be exercised more wisely if fewer persons were held responsible to the electorate.[14] Finally, there developed vast bureaucratic, publicly sponsored welfare services that replaced the services of precinct and ward committeemen in local parties.[15]

"Good government," however, neutralized some very important sources of civic accountability in "machine politics." When public servants were enmeshed in the local political system of cities, they had to be fairly responsive to the demands of citizens because their continuation in office depended upon a local electorate. This was particularly true for members of the lower-middle class and for immigrants to our cities. Indeed, the successive waves of immigrant domination of sectors of public service, such as that of the Germans and Irish in police departments, rested less on merit than on the responsiveness of local government organization to the organized political pressures of each successive wave of immigrants.[16] Local politics in the nineteenth century often brought about the rapid movement of immigrants into positions in the urban polity, who could represent their own interests. Furthermore, the local political organization often served quite effectively as a channel for grievance.[17] The decline of "machine politics" carried with it some measure of loss of accountability on the part of public officials and ser-

14. An excellent account of recruitment, promotion, and tenure of chiefs as well as of officers in St. Louis is found in John K. Maniha, "The Mobility of Elites in a Bureaucratizing Organization: The St. Louis Police Department, 1861–1961" (Ph.D. diss., University of Michigan, 1970).

15. For a good account of this transition from machine politics to party politics, see Elmer E. Cornwell, Jr., "Bosses, Machines and Ethnic Groups," *Annals of the American Academy of Political and Social Science* (May 1964).

16. See James Q. Wilson, "Generation and Ethnic Differences Among Career Police Officers," *The American Journal of Sociology* 69 (March 1964): 522–58.

17. See Nathan Glazer, *Beyond the Melting Pot* (Cambridge: M.I.T. Press, 1963).

vants to citizens and local community-interest groups. The current desire of the lower classes and minorities for local control of centralized municipal bureaucracies, including the police, derives in part from these major changes in local political accountability.

Our current system of civic accountability for organizations in local government is built primarily upon three assumptions: (1) that we can make elected officials responsible for the conduct of officers and servants in the bureaucracies under them; (2) that each bureaucracy establishes effective machinery for handling citizen complaints and insuring justice; and (3) that civil servants are responsive to the public. Over and above this, citizens may seek redress from the legal system by such means as initiating civil suits against public agencies or officials for damages, seeking a warrant from the prosecutor for criminal violations, or obtaining a writ of mandamus.[18] These are questionable assumptions about how any of our many public agencies including law enforcement can be made responsive and responsible to the citizens they serve.

Moreover, although bureaucracy is one of the major ways to assure citizens that public officials exercise discretion in their interests, it also substantially reduces the capacity of citizens and local interest groups to hold these officials accountable. Bureaucracies protect citizen interest by insuring that universalism, legality, and neutrality will govern discretionary decisions by public officials and civil servants. But, these very elements also tend to neutralize civic power. Attempts by citizens to hold police officers accountable for their behavior runs a collision course with an internal accountability system that maintains police personnel are best qualified to evaluate and sanction police conduct. Attempts

18. Writs of Mandamus are rarely issued against the police, because the courts regard law-enforcement activity to require ministerial discretion for its performance, and, therefore, one for which mandamus is inappropriate.

to change the composition of the force or to alter the promotion system of a police department in the public interest encounters resistance from a civil service system of selection and promotion through merit. The combination of police union contracts restricting lateral entry into the department, civil service tests and rankings as the major basis for promotion, and the tendency of the courts to affirm traditional promotional practices have been major bulwarks against the entry of blacks into metropolitan American police departments. The few American police departments—such as those in Chicago, Philadelphia, and Washington—that have significant proportions of black officers in their departments achieved this only when substantial local political interests were called upon to neutralize the bureaucracies. Indeed, the less bureaucratized the police at the local level, the more responsive they are to civic and political power. Many local sheriffs in the United States still stand as testimony to this relationship.

Given the tendency for police bureaucracies to neutralize civic power, how can citizens in modern democratic societies hold bureaucracies like the police accountable? Accountability, it is agreed, must rest in structures, organizations, and processes that are both external and internal to bureaucracies.

Accountability of Police Bureaucracies to External Units

Any bureaucratic organization must be judged from the perspective of its actual and potential clients. Both complaints about service rendered and demands for service to which the agency is not responsive therefore are client concerns. Consider first how the typical system for making and processing complaints appears to the citizen making a complaint to a local bureaucracy such as the police. Begin with the requirement that the citizen shall make and pursue the complaint through the very agency against which it is lodged.

A complaint about a police officer is expected to be lodged with a police commander. Complaints about school teachers should go to school officials and complaints about welfare services must be directed to the welfare agency. Citizens apparently are conditioned to this logic. A survey we conducted of the problems of Detroit-area citizens asked them where they would turn should they want to complain about treatment by the police. Excluding those who didn't seem to know what they would do because they reported they would never have any reason to complain, more than 7 out of 10 would turn first to someone in the police department. Fewer than 1 in 20 would consult an attorney about the matter. No one mentioned addressing his complaint to The Michigan Civil Rights Commission.

Any system whereby complaints are lodged with the guardians of offending parties inevitably coerces many clients against their interests. Many citizens are reluctant to complain against agencies that hold power over them and could respond with punitive action. Furthermore, complaints to agency personnel with an interest in the matter leaves the citizen open to organizational manipulation, which often attempts to "cool" the citizen out of the complaint. In short, the agency is not a disinterested party. Since in our system of justice, justice depends upon "disinterest" in the outcome of a case, it seems obvious that no citizen should be required to make and pursue his complaint through an agency that has a stake in its outcome. To combat much of this neutralization of civic power, the lodging of complaints must be made outside the agency.

Generally some opportunity exists to complain to external agencies, since accountability is lodged with elected officials, or, in criminal violations, with the public prosecutor. Yet it is clear that none of these external agencies is organized to pursue such complaints except on an *ad hoc* basis. There are, however, more compelling reasons why the offices of elected officials should not generally be charged with handling these complaints. Elected public officials can be held responsible for policies governing the operation of a system, but not for individual complaints. Individual complaints require an official authority and organization to receive, process, and decide matters concerning these complaints. Actually, given the political complexion of election to office, officials can be nonresponsive on grounds of political fealty, as the nineteenth-century government of American cities demonstrated.

Lodging the complaint system with the public prosecutor in the existing legal system raises similar questions. Not only is the prosecutor's office poorly organized to develop information on complaints, but prosecutors lack disinterest and accountability in the same sense as do the police. Indeed, for citizen complaints about the police involving a criminal charge against the citizen, the prosecutor may have an interest in maintaining the façade of police propriety, because he has a vested interest in bringing the defendant to trial.[19]

Again, the interests of justice appear to require that complaints be made to sources outside the particular agency that is the object of the complaint. However, there are grounds for questioning whether a disinterested agency should also process complaints and decide about sanctions, since there is evidence that these matters cannot be dealt with as effectively outside the agency that is the object of the complaint.

Citizen complaints against the police, not unlike many complaints lodged in the legal system, often fail of decision because sufficient or adequate evidence is lacking. Moreover, if legal procedure is followed in hearing and deciding complaints, they may fail on procedural grounds. Failure to decide many citizen complaints about the police is understandable, because often the only available evidence is in conflicting oral testimony by officers and complainants. Although studies of the undue use of force by the police show

19. Chevigny, chap. 15.

that others may be present, they rarely are disinterested parties. Generally either fellow police officers or fellow offenders, whose truthfulness can easily be challenged, are the only available witnesses.[20] The difficulty of securing viable witnesses is shown in Paul Chevigny's analysis of citizen complaints against New York City police officers, where attempts were made to prosecute in the courts and to bring the officers before the Review Board of the New York City Police Department. All too often the decision to prosecute or to conduct a review cannot proceed until charges against the complainant and bargaining over civil liability as well as criminal charges have been decided.[21]

The fact that many individual complaints must fail of resolution in any formal legal or procedural sense does not rule out the use of informal means of adjudication. An apology by an officer is all that some citizens require to redress moral indignation over an officer's behavior.[22] Support for the opinion that the evidence from citizen complaints lends itself more to informal adjudication than to formal decisions is found in studies of agencies that specialize in adjudicating complaints. Mayhew's study of the Massachusetts Commission Against Discrimination documents the truth of this for citizen complaints about discrimination, demonstrating that adjudication necessarily became the most common practice.[23] For quite similar reasons the Swedish ombudsman, contrary to popular belief in the United States, uses knowledge gained from complaints to change practices of agencies rather than adjudicate individual complaints. The Swedish and American approaches to processing complaints against officials in bureaucracies provide an interesting contrast.

20. See Albert J. Reiss, Jr., "Police Brutality—Answers to Key Questions" 5 *Trans-action* (July-August, 1968), 10–19.
21. Chevigny, chap. 15.
22. See, for example, Algernon Black, *The People and The Police* (New York: McGraw Hill, 1968).
23. Leon Mayhew, Law and Equal Opportunity (Cambridge: Harvard University Press, 1968).

Emphasis in this country centers on assessing the motivations of individuals, the facts surrounding the alleged misconduct, and adjudication of the case. Thus, Americans would release or punish police officers after hearing and deciding individual complaints. The emphasis of the ombudsman is on changing the structural sources of misconduct, since he is empowered to negotiate for changes in the bureaucracy to *forestall* future occurrences.[24]

Of course there is the problem that handling individual complaints requires an investigative staff, but the real problem concerns the competence of investigators and who should be responsible for investigating.

Most complaints about police behavior challenge their exercise of discretion. This frequently involves the discretion to threaten or use force or to invoke detention and investigation. At issue then, for the police, is who will judge whether discretion was exercised properly. Since professionals regard it as their right to exercise considerable discretion in making decisions about clients, they commonly argue that any review of professional discretion must be made by professionals, if the integrity of the profession is to be protected. To the degree that professionalization of the police is desired, this argument must be considered. The problem is whether the prerogatives and responsibility of professionals shall be granted to the police.

The foregoing discussion poses some of the classic problems in the balancing of interests. The interests of professionals and administrators in the agency to make decisions about the quality of work and to sanction deviation from professional standards must be balanced with citizen concern for proper practice and a right to hold practitioners account-

24. Donald C. Rowat, *The Ombudsman: Citizen's Defender* (London: George Allen & Unwin, 1965), pp. 22–44. Also conversation with the Hon. Alfred Bexilius, Sweden's Ombudsman for Civil Affairs in 1968. See also, Walter Gellhorn, *Ombudsmen and Others: Citizens' Protectors in Nine Countries* (Cambridge: Harvard University Press, 1966).

able to them. One way to balance these interests is to lodge the responsibility for investigation of the complaint, sanctioning of any offending parties, and adjudication in the agency against which the complaint is lodged, while an independent agency would receive all complaints, transmit them to the appropriate agency, and be given a full transcript and report of decisions as to the outcome of investigations. The independent agency then operates as a public accounting agency with the power to communicate all information to citizens and to mobilize the public to press for justice and service to citizens.

There are several reasons for maintaining the investigative and sanctioning functions within the agency. There is the contention, already stated, that professional responsibility requires investigation and sanctioning by peers who alone are capable to evaluate what is the proper exercise of discretion. There is also the argument that professionals will cooperate more fully with internal investigators. Moreover, it often is maintained that change is more likely to result if the administration and the staff of an organization are involved in the investigation and evaluation that recommends change. However, there also are arguments against lodging responsibility for these matters with an offending agency, usually on the grounds that it opens the way for the agency to manipulate matters in its own interest and that citizens are reluctant to cooperate in investigation with an agency against which they have lodged a complaint.

Whatever the stance taken on where to lodge these functions, it is clear that the agency which receives and registers complaints should maintain full control over them to the extent that it receives a full report on the investigation, the actions taken against any offending parties, and on steps for administrative implementation to prevent future occurrences of that kind. Acquisition of the input and output information is one of the most powerful monitoring devices available over an organization. Whoever has that information has the potentiality to assess where the problems of the organization lie. Perhaps one reason why agencies in the criminal-justice system have had so little accountability to their public is because they maintain tight control over their own information. As a matter of fact, of all the agencies in the criminal-justice system, the public prosecutor is least accountable, partly because he rarely releases any aggregative information on his organization.

The power of aggregative information is considerable. The patterns exhibited in matters surrounding the complaint and its processing provide useful information for changing the organization. Characteristically, legalists, journalists, and moral entrepreneurs want to change organizations by making "a case." Usually that means they want to bring action against an individual, group, or organization as adversaries, or at most, press for an adjudication of the matters in the particular case to the satisfaction of offended parties. That may be good public relations; it is hardly good organizational practice. All too often it leaves the agency and its practices unchanged. Generally, the aggregative effects of complaints are more readily discernible and demonstrable than are the merits of an individual case. It is far more difficult to prove that a police department has discriminated against a particular black applicant for employment than to show that the effect of its practices in the aggregate are discriminatory against blacks. A single complaint against an officer for misconduct is easily dismissed but a large number of complaints against him requires administrative attention regardless of the merits of any case.

Another way to balance interests is to create an audit bureau that is independent of the police department. An audit bureau can monitor police work by maintaining continuous audits of the work of officers, conducting investigations of their input and output. Monitoring by this means clearly entails observing how policemen work with citizens and interviewing citizens to determine how officers deal with them and their problems when policing everyday life. Audit bureaus can build confidence in their audit by having teams of citizens and police officers investigate and monitor the work of officers in the department.[25] Such teams might reasonably be part of any community action program.

There are problems in insuring that citizens will register their complaints in ways that will affect the offending agency. One difficulty is the fact that many citizens lack information on *where* to take their complaints. A survey of Detroit-area citizens shows that, when they wish to complain, most citizens don't, because they don't know where to go. When they do complain, they usually turn to the supervisor of the agency against which the complaint is to be lodged. A minority of complainants seek the advice of a lawyer or attempt to arouse the interest of an elected official.[26] Almost all Detroit citizens lacked information on agencies that specialized in handling civil rights complaints. Few people knew about the Michigan Civil Rights Commission or the Detroit Human Relations Commission, agencies that specialize in receiving and processing these complaints. More knew that the Better Business Bureau of the Detroit Chamber of Commerce handled complaints about consumer problems, and most knew about the Action Line columns in the daily newspapers. This lack of information about complaint agencies suggests that it is difficult to disseminate information about the type of complaints an agency specializes in handling. It seems inadvisable then to establish an agency which specializes solely in receiving or monitoring complaints about the police. Rather, what is needed is one agency (or at the most a few) that links citizens effectively to complaint systems. The problem is an organizational one. Citizens should not be required to link their complaints to a whole variety of complaint re-

25. There is an annual audit of crime reporting in the St. Louis, Mo. Police Department that is conducted jointly by the department and an independent Bureau of Government Research.
26. Leon Mayhew and Albert J. Reiss, Jr., "The Detroit Area Study" (Department of Sociology, University of Michigan, 1968).

ceiving and processing agencies. This should be the responsibility of an organization that specializes not only in receiving complaints but also in aiding the citizen in the preparation and forwarding of the complaint to the appropriate agency for action and response.[27]

One may reasonably ask whether the independence of the complaint receiving or auditing agency can be guaranteed, and, ultimately, to whom such agencies are to be held accountable. There is much evidence that agencies reporting to administrative officers or responsible directly to elected or appointed officials are threatened with cooptation by them. They are subject to subversion from interest groups as well. The Swedish solution to this problem was to have Parliament elect the chief ombudsman and make that office directly responsible to it.[28] Such a solution is possible with American local government. Within the American system, however, the more common pattern to avoid cooptation has been to establish voluntary agencies of accountability entirely outside of government. The John Howard Association, to hold corrections officials accountable, and the American Civil Liberties Union are examples of such voluntary organizations. To avoid cooptation by the agency or the governing authority to which the complaint bureau is responsible, communities might establish a general complaint-receiving agency as a voluntary organization supported by the "Community Fund."

Accountability of Police Bureaucracies to Internal Units

A basic problem for police bureaucracies, particularly for the commander, is to protect the organization from being

27. There are, of course, additional advantages both politically and administratively to having a single agency that holds all public officials and civil servants accountable to the police that are not discussed here. See President's Commission on Law Enforcement and The Administration of Justice, *Task Force Report: The Police* (Washington, D.C.: USGPO, 1967, chap. 6.
28. Rowat, *The Ombudsman,* part 4.

subverted by police officers. The sources of organizational subversion are diverse. Apart from the ever-present threat of subversion of the entire organization by the political interests of government, police departments face threats of subversion through the political affiliations of their members. Historically, police departments have dealt with this form of subversion by denying active political participation to sworn personnel in the department. However, although they do receive citizen complaints about the political participation of officers, police departments are not organized to secure intelligence about officers' political participation. Indeed, there is a tacit asumption that so long as participation is limited to working within local organizations of the two-party system, it can be ignored. Almost universally, metropolitan police departments preclude any officer from standing for elective office, although, clearly, county sheriffs stand as an exception.

There is a growing body of evidence that police officers in the United States supported radical-right politics in the late 1960s, and particularly those candidates who exploited racial or student unrest.[29] Inasmuch as radical-right political activity increasingly is linked to the Patrolmen's Benevolent Association and other line organizations of the police, police organizations represent conservative political interests. The New York City PBA, for example, allied itself with efforts of the Conservative Party of New York and the John Birch Society to openly campaign for referendum on the Citizens Review Board of New York City.[30] When Mayor Lindsay of New York City asserted the authority of the mayor over the police, exercising the legal right and duty of his office, he was incongruously challenged by the PBA for political intervention. In Detroit and some other cities, the PBA has proposed to bargain collectively for a policeman's "Bill of Rights" to protect officers when citizens lodge complaints against the police. There also is evidence of a movement to

29. Lipset, pp. 78–83.
30. Chevigny, chap. 4.

develop a national bargaining agent for the police that would set standards for policing by all police officers. Indeed more than one head of a PBA has openly announced that the membership would follow its *own* standards of policing. The emergence of collective bargaining by the police over issues of police policy threatens civil control of the police. The public and the department have difficulty in successfully coping with such political activity since at issue are rights in collective bargaining as well.

Police departments also face subversion of their goals when personnel pervert their law-enforcement roles to profit from criminal activity. The bribe and payoff from "honest" citizens and syndicate men are major threats. To cope with subversion, most major police departments screen candidates for appointment and maintain an internal intelligence (or investigation) division to monitor their conduct after appointment. Such divisions normally are operated as a secret service, reporting directly to the chief.

Evidence documenting the effectiveness of internal intelligence units is mixed because these units are beset with major operating problems. Patrolmen's organizations limit their effectiveness by insisting upon due process of law when the police department brings charges against officers for misconduct. Since often the evidence of an internal intelligence unit will be inadmissible in a court of law on procedural grounds (given the use of such means as entrapment by intelligence agents), insistence on due process limits its effectiveness. Indeed, it is a striking fact that many police officers who denounce the decisions of the United States Supreme Court for the protection of citizen rights are among the most vehement in demanding such standards be followed when they personally are open to criminal charges.[31] Closely related to this

31. The Algiers Motel incident in Detroit provides an excellent example of the legal maneuvering that takes place when the police are interrogated by the police on criminal charges. See John Hersey, *The Algiers Motel Incident* (New York: Alfred A. Knopf, 1968). The second lecture provides examples for cases of investigation by units outside the department.

problem is the matter of maintaining the secret identity of
the investigating officers, a problem not unrelated to bringing
charges on evidence, since the right to confront one's ac-
cusers has the immediate effect of disclosing identity.

While in democratic societies there is an aversion to maintaining subversive-control agencies, one organizational solution to this problem, if such investigation is to continue as a
part of policing the police, is the establishment of an agency
of investigation outside the department. Major police departments could establish such an investigation division co-
operatively, not unlike Interpol or the investigating agencies
insurance companies form to detect fraud. Failure of local
police units to create an effective interdepartmental agency
to control subversion in their ranks by organized criminal
interests will undoubtedly shift the burden of such control
onto federal authorities.

So far as citizens are concerned, supervision and cooptation of police by local political and criminal interests
may seem to be a less crucial problem than the lack of accountability for police behavior toward citizens in everyday
life. The organizational requirements for policing everyday
life explain why police commanders have difficulty preventing individual officers from subverting the goals of the department. The quantity and quality of police behavior at
work are commonly controlled by a system of work supervision. Most work situations in industrial settings involve immediate contact between a supervisor and employees who
work together. This is not usually possible in police work.
Most policing of everyday life occurs when one or more citizens encounter one or more police officers in a social setting
removed from immediate contact with a supervisor.

Assuming an unwillingness to allocate resources for almost one-to-one supervision, the problem for police commanders is to make policemen behave properly when they
are not under supervision. This may be done in several ways.
One means to assess the quality of work would be to set per-

formance criteria that can be objectively evaluated once the work is completed. But, generally this would only apply to the kind and volume of work produced by the officer in oral and written reports. Inasmuch as these reports are produced by the officer, he soon learns to subvert this means by reporting only in terms of the "preferred" performance criteria, whether or not it accords with fact. Moreover, it is inherently difficult to assess conduct in discrete situations without direct observation such as supervision provides.

A second means of evaluation would be to program both supervision and assessment on a selective basis, preferably so an officer could not predict its occurrence. Many agencies develop internal audit units that regularly and systematically sample transactions with clients both as they occur and after services have been completed. This dual audit permits the agency to assess the adequacy of service from both the administrative and the client point of view. The police department, for example, can program a computer to select a supervising sergeant to observe how officers, also selected by computer, handle situations. In addition, it can be programmed to arrange for a supervising sergeant or auditor to interview citizens involved in a transaction immediately after the police have completed their work. Since the computer selects such cases, it is difficult to "beat the system" by controlling selection. To limit the likelihood that the police officers will coopt sergeants and other employees so that audits will generally be favorable to them, the department can employ the services of an independent audit firm. As noted earlier, such audits may well build public confidence in the system and at the same time provide the police administrators with an assessment of performance within their agency.

The third possibility is to control the conduct of the officer by training him to respond to internal standards of performance in keeping with the ethics of a practice. We have identified this latter model with professionalization of an occupation. Adherence to professional responsibility requires not only that the officer be given a task and responsibility for it but also that he sense autonomy and responsibility for the exercise in discretion. To attain this model of professionalization, considerable reorganization and redefinition of police work and of control over discretion in the legal system must be carried out. If the system continually erodes the judgment exercised by officers, there is little incentive to conform to professional standards of performance. Moreover, professionalization of the police occupation will require a shift in the model of supervision and assessment. The balancing of autonomy with supervision and review is no simple matter, particularly if the interests of the client remain at the core of the system. Nevertheless, historically, the best way we have found to control standards of performance in work, apart from direct supervision, is through the professionalization of workers. With increasing professionalization of police work, some of the problems of police malpractice may be solved.

The most modernized police departments opt to a degree for all three models. They require the officer to keep in touch with the communications center and submit reports that can be evaluated. However, all they can ordinarily assess in this way is the degree to which the officer can meet official expectations, and not necessarily how he behaved. Many departments also provide for occasional supervision of police work in on-duty situations, but there is usually no standard assessment procedure for them to follow and records are not systematically kept on the supervision of each officer. Departments attempt to inculcate an ethic of proper police conduct by stressing obligation to duty. Yet the volume of citizen complaints about police misconduct—evidence that at least a sizeable proportion of such complaints are justified—and the infrequent application of sanctions for violations show that current organizational controls provide an inadequate level of internal accountability.

Mechanisms to Enhance Accountability

Much of the concern about making the police accountable for their conduct toward citizens is directed toward the adjudication of complaints about officer misconduct. The object is to satisfy particular citizens and their friends, thereby stabilizing the organization by protecting it from any political acts on the parts of the disaffected. A secondary goal in adjudication may be to warn officers to "keep their noses clean." On the other hand, citizen complaints may be treated as symptoms of organizational problems, thereby making them a potential basis for changing administrative structure, policies, or practices.

Given the essentially adversary character of most proceedings about police malpractice or misconduct, a judgment is reached for any particular case that includes a finding of fact, some evaluation of the officer's responsibility, and whether or not he should be sanctioned negatively. As noted previously, most review procedures generally conclude the complaint was not justified, and the officer is exonerated. If incriminated in some way, he is usually "let off" with a reprimand or required to pay a small fine. The overall procedure for handling complaints may include some feedback to the citizen to satisfy him that something has been done, but that is all.

What is lacking in such a system of processing complaints is a method to protect the long-run interests of both officers and citizens. Such methods could be effected through changes in the internal proceedings of police departments. Consider first how the use of findings from the review might be changed. There are many ways that police administrators and officials in the system of criminal justice could utilize complaints about officer practices as a basis for *education* of the officer. Supervision and auditing of an officer's behavior could be used to assist the officer in increasing his skill rather

than to punish him for bad practice. Feedback as education
has the great advantage of reinforcing desirable behavior in
police practice. In a similar vein, the prosecutor and the
judge could explain to the officers how matters might be
handled in the future rather than scold them or deny them
cases because of poor practice.

Other changes in the nature of internal proceedings of review seem worthy of consideration. At the present time, review proceedings are surrounded by a great deal of secrecy,
largely unwarranted. When it is warranted, it is generally
temporarily so, awaiting the resolution of criminal charges
in the criminal courts. To be sure, in the interest of justice,
the rights of defendants and plaintiffs must be protected in
proceedings. But the proceeding itself and any decisions
resulting from it need not be privileged information. Complainants as well as responsible agencies within the community are entitled to a full report of the proceedings,
decisions, and actions based on them with respect to all complaints. Accountability in a democratic society requires that
a citizen's complaint cannot become the property of the very
agency against which the complaint is lodged.

Continual review of the behavior of all police in all encounters with citizens is an ideal mechanism to insure that
officers meet standards of practice. While such a mechanism
is ordinarily costly and inefficient, there are approximations
to continual review. One of these would require that the police issue each citizen a receipt for any police-work contact.[32] It seems anomalous that in our society only a police
officer who contacts a citizen in an offense involving an automobile discloses his identity and provides the citizen with a
record of the place of contact and the charge. In some states,
such as Florida, the practice is extended to the issuance of

32. Several police departments, New York City and New Orleans,
for example, issue "citizen identification" (CI) forms for some police
encounters. New Orleans issues them to about one-sixth of all citizens
who are stopped and frisked.

warning tickets which indicate only that the violator is held accountable by a warning.

Citizens are not even provided with an official document of police contact at the time of arrest or booking. Police departments have become quite sophisticated about the control of traffic warrants, using them as an index of accountability and to maintain a level of enforcement. Such practice could easily be extended to include any contact between law-enforcement agents and members of the public. Where there is any contact between a police officer in his role as *law-enforcement agent* and a member of the public, the officer could be obligated to provide the citizen with an official notice or receipt of the encounter. Such official notices or receipts could cover all classes of official contact, not just a restricted set such as all arrests.

Police officers should be required to make an official record of *any* work contact with a citizen when the encounter is terminated, whether or not an arrest is made. Immediately on completion, a copy of the form should be given to the citizen as an official notice acknowledging the contact, and another copy should be filed with the department. The form must be numbered uniquely, as it is for traffic warrants, to insure greater accountability in its use.

Just what the form should include is not altogether set. The following items of information seem necessary: (1) name and address of citizen(s) with whom an official contact is made; (2) star number or name of the officer; (3) location of contact, and whether or not an automobile was involved; (4) reason for contact, the date, hour, and length of time of the contact; (5) a statement of the rights of the citizen in contacts with law-enforcement officers and a statement that these rights were communicated to the citizen; (6) a notice advising the citizen that, for any questions or complaints about the contact, he may call a central number, write to a particular department office, or appear in person at a given office; (7) any special features of the decision related either to the officer's discretion or the citizen's options, e.g., a citizen's inability to communicate with an officer, and why, or a citizen's refusal to sign a complaint.

A citizen's receipt for contact with the police could benefit both citizens and the police command. Citizens would have the protection afforded by any official document. And, they could insist on such a receipt, thereby increasing the likelihood that the police will be governed by legality in their relations with citizens. Since the receipt would also provide citizens with information on how to proceed with any complaint they might have about the contact, or about the manner in which the officer executed the receipt, it would increase the accountability of officers in the department. The police command could use the information to assess officer performance. And, furthermore, such records would increase the administrator's span of control over the behavior of officers.

It is important that the citizen be given a receipt immediately on completion of an encounter. If an arrest is made in a field setting, it should be given at the time of the arrest. The purpose of the receipt is to protect the citizen from continual alteration of "official" records in the interest of bureaucracy. Indeed, citizens should be given a receipt each time any officer exercises discretion in his case and at every turning point in processing him as a person. Discretionary acts such as those of booking, charging, setting conditions of release, detention, plea bargaining, and adjudication all must be receipted to citizens if the system, not just the police, is ultimately to be held accountable.

The main arguments against this proposal are easily anticipated, and most of them turn out on examination to lack substance. One argument might be that it would cost too much money, but it would cost less than school reports to parents. Superficially, it can be argued that the receipt infringes further upon the liberties of citizens by creating a police file of information on citizens that can be misused.

All information, of course, can be misused. In truth, nothing now protects the citizen against any such information entering into police files! The problem is how to protect citizens from the misuse of information, not the gathering of information *lest* it be misused.

Debureaucratization and Civic Accountability

There is a growing restiveness in American society, particularly among the lower classes, with bureaucratic neutralization of civic power, represented by the inability of many citizens to affect policies and practices in central bureaucracies. There should be little doubt that most central bureaucracies, including the police, have been slow to respond to pressures—at least those from minorities and the poor in our cities—to change policies and practices. A movement is under way in many larger cities to neutralize the power of the central bureaucracies by breaking up administrative control and decentralizing decision making to local units. A major strategy is to develop more autonomous administrative units within the central bureaucracy that are subject to control by the clients of the bureaucracy.

The breaking up of the administrative power of the central bureaucracy poses a serious challenge to its model of rational control. Clearly at issue for the central bureaucracy is how can civic power be used to make central bureaucracies accountable to the citizens they serve. I assume that, at least theoretically, an increase in civic power is possible without restructuring the central bureaucracy into semi-autonomous local units. I assume also that proposals to decentralize police bureaucracies want to do more than enhance the participation of *some* citizens in the organization. Rather, these proposals really aim at gaining local control of all administrative decisions that affect clients in the local agency or area. The discussion that follows, therefore, considers some of the consequences anticipated if reasonably autonomous local units under the control of local citizens are created to police everyday life.

The history of police organizations, where a rational central bureaucracy with central command and control emerged to destroy the feudality of local precinct commands, together with the history of law enforcement in our rural communities, where feudal relations predominate, should engender skepticism about the breaking up of central police bureaucracies. A review of past problems stemming from local control, as well as a statement of some likely consequences of local autonomy and control for police in our large cities, may help in evaluating any proposal to decentralize administrative control in police bureaucracies to local jurisdictions.

One of the more difficult problems in policing is the development of policy that is consistent with the democratic ideology of maintaining respect for the rule of law. The law requires universality in its application, but community standards often hold it should be otherwise. Whenever citizens are subject to widely varying standards in the application of any law, they lose respect for it and for the rule of law. Local control of police policy and practice, therefore, runs the risk of undermining the rule of law.

The establishment of many autonomous local jurisdictions within a metropolitan area is, in many ways, incompatible with the goals of a free society. As noted earlier, while local control of police may offer protection from a police state, paradoxically, it opens the door to local tyranny, including the tyranny of local police. Within major metropolitan areas of our country today, suburban jurisdictions surround the metropolis with local police jurisdictions. Many have a feudal character with the police enforcing local standards of pride and prejudice. In "Whitey's" suburbs there also are "Whitey's" police. The creation of local police jurisdictions within a city would only exaggerate racial and class barriers, because the city is nothing more than a mosaic of race and class. Consider, for instance, what kind of policing might exist in poor white and poor black areas adjacent to one another in the city. Were each to develop its own "race of police" and set its own standards of policing, the free movement of citizens might easily be restricted by their exercise of discretion. Only a central bureaucracy can override community standards that are not in the public interest, because its rational model of control applies standards universally.

At the heart of proposals for local community control of central bureaucracies are conceptions of community, community standards, citizen participation, and community power that fail to confront the realities of urban life and organization. Conceptions of community and of community standards all too often assume homogeneity and stability of the population that does not exist in most local areas of the metropolis. Many police precincts are characterized by a diversity of peoples. Differences in age, race, class, and other interests within a population often mean differences in expectations about what standards of behavior and law enforcement should prevail in the community. "Community" frequently means conflicting rather than common interests. Businessmen may want the police to keep young people from loitering before and about their places of business. Residents who park their cars in the street may resent young residents playing there and call the police. Local moral entrepreneurs may insist that the police enforce the gambling statutes or closing hours for night life contrary to the wishes of other residents. Indeed, the police know they are called to handle disputes among citizens precisely because there are differences about standards of behavior and law enforcement within their precinct. They recognize cleavage more often than consensus is the starting point for policy.

Conceptions of citizen participation in the community may rest on false assumptions about the stability of the population. When more than 1 in 5 residents of the city each year changes place of residence, the long-run interest of residents is served by insuring that the police will behave in a prescribed manner no matter where the citizen lives in the city. It is extremely doubtful, for instance, that local precinct police would have protected the interests of Negroes as they moved into areas formerly segregated on the basis of race. Yet it was possible for centralized police commands to protect the interests of those who led in the racial desegregation of housing.[33]

Citizens are very vulnerable to control by special interests within the community. Moreover, precinct police are vulnerable to subversion by criminal interests, as the commanders of central bureaucracies are only too aware. There is little reason to expect that local citizens can control the effect that larger organized interests in crime will have on them or their police, given the difficulty central metropolitan police jurisdictions have had in controlling the subversion of police in the precincts.

Moreover, the participation of citizens in any community is invariably channeled into political representation by organized groups in the community. Local interest groups, once entrenched in power roles, can and do become more resistant to change than do incumbents in roles of the central bureaucracy. It is far easier for the central bureaucracy to dislodge the local precinct commanders or any officers by simply transferring them than it is for the local community to remove them from office. Indeed, local autonomy in police recruitment and training could easily lower the ceiling on professionalization and mobility of the police, thereby thwarting the development of a professional police cadre.

33. See Joseph D. Lohman, et al., *Segregation in the Nation's Capitol* (Washington, D.C.: National Committee on Segregation in the Nation's Capitol, November 1948); and Joseph D. Lohman and Dietrich C. Reitzes, "Note on Race Relations in Mass Society," *The American Journal of Sociology* 58 (November 1952): 240–47.

There is a substantial risk that local political control will become merely a substitute for central bureaucratic control. Neither central nor local control guarantees or thwarts broad citizen participation in government or the nature of the accountability of the agency to citizens. In fact, the problems of citizen participation commonly phrased as "participatory democracy" and "direct involvement of citizens in decision making" are often false issues. In democratic societies, more often than not, the problem is one of how public and private organizations can be held accountable to all citizens rather than how citizens can participate in the decisions that are made. Where individual citizens are involved, neither their fate nor their influence should rest on so ephemeral a matter as who participates in a particular decision. In mass democratic societies, the central problem for citizens is how they may be brought closer to the centers of political power that control the acquisition and allocation of resources, not whether administrative control is centralized or decentralized in the bureaucracy.

Proposals to establish local police commands under the control of local citizens fail to take into account the fact that local power cannot solve many of the issues that the central bureaucracy is criticized for handling ineffectively. Local control may in fact exacerbate them. What is more, when civic power is mobilized on behalf of the central bureaucracy, the capacity of both to resolve the issues is usually greater. Even more to the point, the local community often cannot generate the resources that are necessary to deal with the local issues. To shift to citizen participation in administration does not solve the problem of acquiring and allocating resources among the different community units. That problem is dealt with by political organization and administrative policies. Local power depends primarily in joining with other jurisdictions to form power blocs which can generate and allocate resources.

It is anomalous that the ineffectiveness of local citizen

groups in mobilizing civic power to change central bureaucracies is used as an argument to organize these groups to
themselves resolve matters which they usually depend
upon central government and bureaucracies to deal with. If
local power is sufficient to break up central bureaucracies,
is it not sufficient to alter them without their fragmentation
into semiautonomous units?

Punishing Police Behavior

Anyone familiar with police departments becomes aware
of the fact that the official means of sanctioning behavior is
dominated more by punishments than rewards. Although
awards are given for bravery or exceptional performance in
the line of duty, the policing of everyday life is surprisingly
devoid of such occasions. The means of official punishment
also are fairly limited, ranging from primarily suspension
with or without loss of pay to outright dismissal from the
department. Official punishments are deprivations visited
not only upon the man but on the department and his family
as well.

The day-to-day relations among superiors and men in the
line are dominated by an informal set of rewards and punishments. Superiors manipulate the system through controlling
the assignment of work, e.g., assigning the "dirty work" as
punishment. Informal sanctions are often exercised by
transferring men within the department; sending officers to
the least desirable precincts. In truth, slum police precincts,
like slum schools, become the repository of those who are
in trouble with the command in the department.

Much of the research on human behavior demonstrates
that punishment is a poor way to get people to conform to a
standard of conduct. More often than not punishment systems are self-defeating, encouraging elaborate procedures
to circumvent them. The most common way to circumvent
punishment is to develop a subculture that deprives mem-

bers of status among their peers if they cooperate with those who operate the system of punishment. Under extreme circumstances, the subcultural groups may even mete out severe punishments to those who cooperate with authorities. They invariably do so when the cost of cooperation threatens the position of everyone in the system. Police subculture rewards men for withholding information and evidence from their superiors when one of their number is to be punished.

The subcultural norm against testifying or offering information against a fellow officer is one of the strongest in the subculture, holding as strongly for internal as for external investigations. The subcultural price for violating this norm is absolute exclusion from the informal life of officers and a refusal by all officers to work with the officer who "cops out." The latter has the devastating effect of getting superiors to carry out this ultimate punishment of banishment by ordering removal of the officer for "failure to get along with his fellow officers." Indeed, it is as unlikely for one police officer to testify against another as it is for one student to testify that another has cheated in a classroom situation. The parallels between officer and student subcultures is not without sociological reason. Each is in a system where there is a high investment in evaluating individual performance. Infractions among officers and students are fairly common so that the exposure of one may expose others. Since each may potentially be harmed, each has an investment in subverting the system of evaluation and information regarding deviation from this system. Both officers and students develop a subculture that prohibits testimony about misconduct precisely because the penalties that dominate the system may jeopardize a life career by banishment.

The famed blue curtain between men in the line and their staff and between the police and the public derives in large part from their system of punishment. This system hinders effective investigation and review procedures within the department, and, outside the department, it hinders the development of effective accountability and legitimate practice toward citizens.

It often seems unnecessary to punish either police or students for their misconduct, because there are alternative ways to handle misconduct. So far as the police are concerned, a sanction that necessitates further training may be far more effective than one that removes the officer from training. A transfer of duty without concomitant loss of status is probably more effective than one that deprives an officer of status. Where the misconduct may disqualify an officer for police work, it need not result in outright dismissal. A municipal bureaucracy has many different jobs for which an officer should be able to qualify. In many cases, it may be possible to transfer officers without loss of pay and seniority based on length of service. A recognition that disqualification for police work need not punish a man and his family should make it possible to develop a more helpful system of appraising behavior within the department. If the findings of behavioral science research are valid, alternatives to punishment should substantially decrease the features of occupational culture that are hostile to public accountability for behavior.

The Legitimacy of Police Authority and Citizen Respect for the Police

The fact that police are locally organized and controlled in a society does not necessarily imply that they are highly integrated with the local populace. Much depends upon the general cultural support legitimating their activity and the patterns of deference and demeanor obtained in the society. The police and the public in England and the United States provide an interesting contrast in these respects. The English police (other than the London Metropolitan Police), like those in the United States, are essentially local, though they are loosely linked by a central inspection system and receive some fiscal support from the national treasury.[34] In England, the police and public rely almost as much on custom as on legal institutions to govern the relationship between the police and the populace.[35] Some years ago, for example, it was reported in England that the "underworld" rapidly produced the offenders who shot three police officers, obviously a crime as much against custom as against a legal norm. Whether or not the underworld was shocked out of custom is immaterial; the public was. The police in England can count upon a whole host of customary patterns that affirm the legitimacy of their role. Police work in the United States, by contrast, is regarded as a work role legitimated by legal institutions. Even members of legal organizations in the United States, such as the courts, are more likely to punish than to praise police officers for their behavior. The police in the United States have occupational prestige. They do not have status honor.[36] The fact that custom does not support the police in the United States means that legal institutions are used to formally restrict police authority with citizens, a not uncommon solution in the absence of custom. Today, in the United States, the police are formally more restricted in their relations with citizens than are the police in England.

While cultural homogeneity of populations, institutional forms of legitimacy in the society, and even national histories produce differences in customary behavior with the police and legal control of them, there are other reasons as well. In the absence of custom, systems of local control are subject to extralocal control in a democratic society such as

34. Federal legislation of the past few years in the United States now brings fiscal support for the local police. In all likelihood, such support in the United States, as in England, will be increasingly available only through demonstration of standards of performance by the local police.
35. See Banton, chaps. 4 and 8.
36. See David J. Bordua and Albert J. Reiss, Jr., "Command, Control and Charisma: Reflections on Police Bureaucracy," *The American Journal of Sociology* 72 (July, 1966): 75–76.

the United States. This control is based largely on political authority through state or federal legislation and constitutional authority exercised through judicial decisions.

The relatively smaller role in the United States of customary relations supporting the legitimacy of police relations with citizens, and vice versa, creates problems concerning how much authority should reside in local as opposed to state or federal government. Ambivalent as American citizens often are toward federal authority, the history of attempts to control crime and policing in the United States is one of increasing assertion of federal authority in such matters. This is reflected both in the growth of federal legislation with a concomitant increase in the size of federal police organizations, such as the FBI, the Bureau of Narcotics Enforcement, and the United States Treasury, and in the increasing number of criminal cases that raise constitutional issues, are appealed, and decided by the United States Supreme Court.

The pluralistic legislative and judicial system of the United States means that federal legislators and jurists often override state and local authority. Both federal and legislative solutions to the "crime problem" in the United States bring with them enormous consequences for the policing of everyday life. The increase in federal laws, as already noted, increases the size of federal enforcement and judicial divisions. As a mark of our civic ambivalence toward a national police force, federal enforcement is not identified with police in the United States. Federal police are euphemistically referred to as agents of law enforcement. Early in 1968, President Nixon's proposal to allocate a large proportion of his recommended increase in the budget for crime control to substantially increase the enforcement of federal laws passed almost without public comment. This included recommendations to substantially increase the number of proactive agents and investigative divisions within the Department of Justice. The number of federal laws that are to be enforced by federal agents in some department of the executive branch grows with each session of Congress. What is surprising is that congressional debate about crime legislation which adds enforcement by national police agents never makes the creation of a national police force an issue. Public stances notwithstanding, the Congress of the United States has developed a national police force of substantial proportions.[37]

While legislative and enforcement provisions are growing at the federal level, judicial decision based on constitutional rather than legislative authority likewise has burgeoned. The effect of the United States Supreme Court's decisions could be far-reaching in controlling police behavior in the United States. Legality, of course, is thereby substituted for custom. The effect of constitutional decisions on the police is generally to limit police discretion under the law. As such, the decisions limit the means or procedures that police use in dealing with citizens rather than the ends of police conduct. Constitutional decisions serve to control, however, only insofar as the police, prosecutors and criminal courts implement them. Constitutional authority is limited if anyone opts not to process a matter in the criminal-justice system. Police conformity with constitutional decisions depends to a substantial degree upon the willingness of police administrators and officers to implement the mandate of the decision. Our studies of police behavior toward citizens in searches of the persons and their property, confessions, and interrogation following the major United States Supreme Court decisions on these matters

37. It is characteristic of American society to back into solutions that are at odds with major elements in its value system. Such solutions, however, always are cloaked in euphemisms that are consistent with the value system. We have Old Age and Survivor's *Insurance*, not taxes, federal *agents*, and not police.

show that often police officers do not conform to these decisions, and their superiors do not sanction them for their failure to do so.[38] The appellate machinery of civic accountability is thus weakened by officer discretion and department policy.

Yet the effect of appellate decisions on police behavior could be considerable through the operation of the exclusionary rule in trial proceedings. The exclusionary rule gives the court the power to exclude any evidence where proper procedure was not followed in acquiring it. Our recent work suggests that the discretion exercised by prosecutors, defense lawyers, defendants, and judges in admitting only a very small percentage of charges to trial undermines the operating foundation of the exclusionary rule. The bargain justice of the prosecutor and the court encouraging the defendant to enter a plea of guilt renders the normative power of the Supreme Court ephemeral. Not only do defendants bargain away a most fundamental right by a plea of guilt, but the prosecutor and the courts also effectively bargain away most of their power to hold the police accountable for their behavior toward citizens.

In America, the concern about police accountability relates almost entirely to the accountability of our local police. Dissatisfaction with the policing of everyday life is far from widespread in our population and the police can count more on citizen support than opposition. Even within major metropolitan areas, organized opposition to the police and demands that they be held accountable are largely, though

38. See Albert J. Reiss, Jr. and Donald J. Black, "Interrogation and the Criminal Process," *The Annals of the American Academy of Political and Social Science* 374 (November 1967): 47–57; and Donald J. Black and Albert J. Reiss, Jr., "Patterns of Behavior in Police and Citizen Transactions," in President's Commission on Law Enforcement and the Administration of Justice, *Studies in Crime and Law Enforcement in Major Metropolitan Areas,* Field Surveys III, vol. 2, sec 1 (Washington, D.C.: USGPO, 1967).

not exclusively, limited to civil rights groups representing minority group interests.[39]

The relatively restricted nature of public criticism of the police in the United States is even more apparent if we consider how much policing remains unquestioned and unconsidered. There are rarely controversies involving our state police, federal agents, and private police.[40] In fact the degree to which these levels of policing remain unquestioned is apparent in the Task Force Report of the Police prepared for the National Crime Commission. Except for brief mention of State police and federal agents, the report drops any consideration of them. There is almost no mention of the vast growth of private policing in the United States under the guise of industrial protection and security or private investigation.[41] And, further, recommendations by the Commission about the police are limited to local police. Recommendations directed to the states, for instance, are directed to the role of the states in controlling local police through legislation and administration, rather than control of the State police.

The extent to which police, other than those in local jurisdictions, are the subject of controversy in America was investigated in one of our Detroit surveys.[42] We told a sample of the metropolitan area residents that sometimes people have problems with the police. We then told them

39. See Albert J. Reiss, Jr., "Career Orientations, Job Satisfaction, and the Assessment of Law Enforcement Problems," in President's Commission on Law Enforcement and the Administration of Justice, *Studies in Crime and Law Enforcement in Major Metropolitan Areas,* Field Surveys III, vol. 2 (Washington, D.C.: USGPO, 1967).

40. There has been some criticism of State police and of the National Guard in policing civil disorders and campus unrest, matters unrelated to the policing of everyday life, however.

41. President's Commission on Law Enforcement and the Administration of Justice, *Task Force Report: The Police* (Washington, D.C.: USGPO, 1967). See esp. pp. 6–7 for the consideration of the state and federal law enforcement.

42. Mayhew and Reiss.

to suppose that a local police officer (and then a Michigan State Police officer, and finally an FBI agent) had not done the right thing when he dealt with them and queried: "Would you do anything about it?" "What would you do?" "To whom would you turn if you wanted something done about it?" and, "What effect do you think that would have?" Clearly, our intent was to explore how citizens would go about making police organizations accountable to them and whether they regarded complaining as having a worthwhile effect. The most interesting finding was that most interviewers and many respondents, from the pretest through the final survey objected to our asking the same questions about the State policemen and FBI agents that were asked about the local police. A majority of respondents readily accepted the idea that they might have problems with the local police, but they either made disclaimers or treated as irrelevant the same questions about State policemen and FBI agents. No doubt, the responses of citizens reflect the fact that their exposure to police officers in everyday life is limited primarily to local police. Equally apparent, however, was their subjective distance from any but the local police. Though much is made of the inhospitability of American citizens to their police, it is clear that most do not believe their State police or federal agents would behave improperly toward them, and therefore their accountability to citizens is not an issue. Distrust of police authority and failure to grant legitimacy to their intervention exists largely where policing is central to everyday life. The policing of everyday life falls to local policemen who, in the jargon of citizens, are invidiously called "cops."

Epilogue

What I have tried to show is that in the long as well as in the short run, a civil police depends upon a civil citizenry. Civility in police and citizen relations is best insured by customary relations and respect for police authority, a reciprocal set of expectations and sanctions, both internal and external systems for holding police accountable to citizens, and a professional police.

Lest anyone conclude that the dependence of a civil police on a civil society is a license for the police to misbehave, it should be clear that it is the responsibility of the government in a democratic society to insure that its servants behave in a civil fashion. The police are not only obliged to behave in a civil way toward citizens but their behavior is strategic in changing relations between citizens and the police. To the degree that we can develop civility in police relations with citizens, we move toward a civil society.

INDEX

Aldrich, Howard, xv, 163
American Civil Liberties Union, 197
Amir, Menachem, 80
Ann Arbor News, 138
Arrest: clearance of crime by, 80, 105, 109, 135; interference with, 55–62; on probable cause, 79, 90, 134; resisting, 55–62, 153. *See also* Police behavior, arrest
Authority: coercive, 46, 150; compliance with, 151, 177–79; legitimacy of police use of, 2–3, 11, 57–62, 64, 116–17, 126, 141–45, 149, 175–80 , 184–85, 214–20; police assertion of, 46–54, 136, 150–51, 175–80; public definitions of, 3, 149, 174; public respect of police, 47, 149, 179

Bacon, Selden, 114
Banton, Michael, 182, 215
Becker, Howard S., 127
Bexelius, Hon. A., 193
Biderman, Albert D., 66, 68
Black, Algernon, 154, 192
Black, Donald, xv, 15, 76, 83, 93, 134, 136, 218
Bordua, David, xv, 2, 150, 215
Bureaucratization: and debureaucratization, 207; defined, 123–24, 188–89; neutraliza-

tion of civic power, 188–89, 207; of police departments, xi, 114–15, 124–25, 128, 168, 181–82, 197–98, 207–08; of professions, 4, 181
Burnham, David, 129

Campbell, Angus, 142
Chevigny, Paul, 149, 154, 155, 184, 191, 192, 198
Christie, Nils, 183
Citizen behavior: aggression toward police, 50–62, 137; on arrest, 55–62, 137; control of police, 65–69, 78–80, 88; deference toward police, 83; 137, 145, 149, 175, 179–81; emotional state in police encounters, 49–51; civility toward police, 11, 48–55, 68, 115, 137–38, 145–49, 184–85
Citizen roles: adversaries, 65, 80, 82, 145; bystanders, 19, 57, 145; complainants, 13–15, 19–21, 58, 64, 77, 83–84, 88, 114, 145; informants, 19, 65, 151; jurors, 116; offenders, 19, 54–62, 145–47; suspects, 19, 145; victims, 64, 69, 83–84; 86–88; witnesses, 69, 79, 81, 116, 135, 145
Civic accountability: by audit bureaus, 195–96; citizen support for, 219–20; external